Swiss

IN WISCONSIN

Revised and Expanded Edition

Frederick Hale

WISCONSIN HISTORICAL SOCIETY PRESS

Published by the
Wisconsin Historical Society Press

www.wisconsinhistory.org

Photographs identified with PH, WHi, or WHS are from the
Society's collections; address inquiries about such photos to the
Visual Materials Archivist at the above address.

Printed in the United States of America
Text and cover designed by Jane Tenenbaum

18 17 16 15 14   2 3 4 5 6

Library of Congress Cataloging-in-Publication Data

Hale, Frederick, 1948–
Swiss in Wisconsin / Frederick Hale.—Rev. and expanded ed.
p. cm.
Includes bibliographical references and index.
ISBN 978-0-87020-377-0 (pbk. : alk. paper)
1. Swiss Americans—Wisconsin—History. 2. Immigrants—Wisconsin—History.
3. Swiss Americans—Wisconsin—Ethnic identity. 4. Swiss Americans—Wisconsin—
Social conditions. 5. New Glarus (Wis.)—History. 6. Wisconsin—History.
7. Wisconsin—Ethnic relations. I. Title.
F590.S9H35 2007
977.50043'5—dc22
2006103067

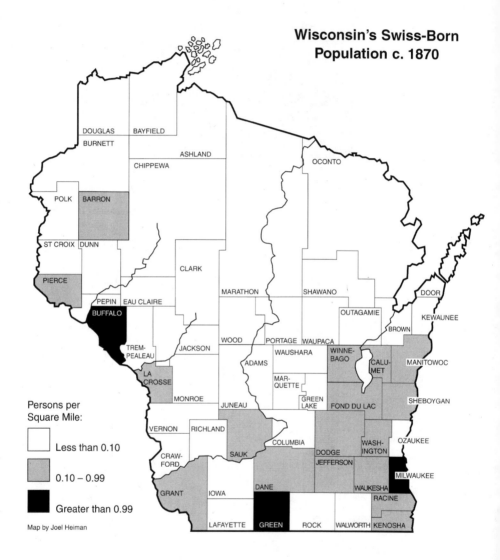

Wisconsin's Swiss-Born Population c. 1870

DOUGLAS
BAYFIELD
BURNETT
ASHLAND
CHIPPEWA
OCONTO
POLK
BARRON
ST CROIX DUNN
CLARK
PIERCE
MARATHON
SHAWANO
DOOR
PEPIN EAU CLAIRE
OUTAGAMIE
KEWAUNEE
BUFFALO
BROWN
WOOD PORTAGE WAUPACA
TREM-
PEALEAU JACKSON
WAUSHARA
WINNE-
BAGO
CALU-
MET
MANITOWOC
ADAMS
LA
CROSSE
MAR-
QUETTE
MONROE
JUNEAU
GREEN
LAKE
FOND DU LAC
SHEBOYGAN
VERNON RICHLAND
COLUMBIA
WASH-
INGTON
OZAUKEE
CRAW-
FORD
SAUK
DODGE
JEFFERSON
MILWAUKEE
GRANT
IOWA
DANE
WAUKESHA
RACINE
LAFAYETTE GREEN ROCK WALWORTH KENOSHA

Persons per Square Mile:

Less than 0.10

0.10 – 0.99

Greater than 0.99

Map by Joel Heiman

A NEW HOME IN NEW GLARUS

As the *Föhn* blew the first breaths of spring into the Alps in March 1845, two Swiss men embarked on a circuitous voyage that took them from the impoverished canton of Glarus in eastern Switzerland to the hills of southern Wisconsin. Their mission was to select and purchase an appropriate tract of land to which the cantonal government could dispatch part of its excess population. Concerned citizens earlier had founded an emigration society and sent inquiries to Swiss consular authorities in the United States as well as in Mexico, Brazil, Russia, and other countries before concluding that what is now the Midwest, a region that had already attracted hundreds of Swiss immigrants, offered the most favorable conditions for creating a new home at least partly reminiscent of the Helvetian fatherland. Having obtained an appropriation from the canton and collected subscriptions from prospective emigrants totaling about $2,600, Nicholas Dürst, a forty-eight-year-old judge, and Fridolin Streiff, a blacksmith nineteen years younger, sailed from Le Havre, France, on March 16 and stepped ashore in New York fifty-two days later.

Heeding instructions, the two proceeded to Easton, Pennsylvania, where a Swiss American named Joshua Frey joined them as their guide. Piecing together a complicated itinerary, which took them across New York, Lake Erie, Michigan, and the southern part of Lake Michigan, the trio arrived in Chicago on May 19 to begin their quest. Knowing that the pre-emption law of 1841 had earmarked for sale vast expanses of the public domain at the bargain price of $1.25 per acre, they called at the United States land office in Chicago, only to learn that little timber acreage remained unclaimed. Dürst, Streiff, and Frey therefore crisscrossed northern Illinois, southern Wisconsin, and parts of Missouri and Iowa inspecting prairie land, open spaces of already proven fertility but dishearteningly unlike the forest-clad hills and jagged peaks of Glarus. On a second visit to Mineral Point in Iowa County, Wisconsin, however,

the three met Theodor and Friedrich Rodolf, Swiss brothers who had settled there in 1834. The Rodolfs offered to assist them in purchasing suitable land at a site near Exeter in Green County, which they had passed
through earlier in the summer. Finally, on July 17, Dürst and Streiff purchased 1,280 acres of timber and prospective farmland on behalf of the
Emigration Society of the Canton of Glarus.

In the meantime, nearly two hundred of the society's other economically stressed members had impatiently advanced their departure from
1846 to April 1845 and had sailed from the Netherlands to Baltimore,
Maryland, where they arrived on June 30. Still unsure of their destina-
tion, they journeyed by way of Pittsburgh and Cincinnati to St. Louis.
Two members of the party set out from there in search of Dürst and
Streiff, finding them hard at work at the site in Green County. One of the
expedition's leaders recorded that it was "beautiful beyond expectation"
and offered "excellent timber, good soil, fine springs, and a stream filled
with fish." Its wildlife, he noted, included large numbers of deer, prairie
chickens, and rabbits.

A week later, on August 15, 1845, their fellow immigrants arrived,
minus several dozen who had either died en route or abandoned the
enterprise to seek their fortunes in Baltimore, Pittsburgh, St. Louis, or
Wheeling, West Virginia. Thus began perhaps the most distinctively
Swiss settlement in the United States, unimaginatively dubbed New
Glarus by its patriotic inhabitants when it was officially organized five
years later.

✌✚✌

WISCONSIN'S FIRST *GLARNER*

This band of *Glarner*, however, were not the first Swiss to settle in the territory of Wisconsin. That honor probably belongs to several immigrants
who had abandoned a colonization venture in Canada. In 1810 a Scottish nobleman, Thomas Douglas, better known as Lord Selkirk, and his
brother-in-law purchased 116,000 square miles of what is now Manitoba
from the Hudson's Bay Company, in which they were the controlling
stockholders. (For purposes of comparison, Wisconsin encompasses a
mere 56,154 square miles.) Lord Selkirk then arranged the settlement of
several groups of evicted Scottish crofters on the domain, the present-day

city of Winnipeg. After enduring the rigors of the Canadian winter, attacks by inhospitable Indians as well as voracious grasshoppers, and a violent struggle with the rival North West Company, many of these Scots deserted their settlement, leaving the experiment in a shambles. Picking up the pieces, Lord Selkirk sent agents to Switzerland, to promote the challenges of the Canadian frontier. More than two hundred venturesome German- and French-speaking Helvetians representing a wide spectrum of occupations sailed to Canada in 1821. Despite a promising start on the land of Lord Selkirk, who had died the previous year, many nearly starved or froze to death the first winter and left for Minnesota at the beginning of the second.

In 1823 another disenchanted band of thirteen families trekked overland and sailed down the Mississippi River to bustling St. Louis in search of tolerable living conditions and economic opportunity. Many soon became dissatisfied with St. Louis and, suffering from ague, returned upstream to the Fever River mining district in Illinois, where they found employment in the lead mines and on neighboring farms. Several of the men were prosperous enough to purchase federal land in present-day Lafayette County in southwestern Wisconsin near Shullsburg and Gratiot, which was named for one of the Swiss families.

This group of Swiss, although reinforced by other families who also left Canada for the Mississippi Valley, were too few in number to maintain much ethnic identity as other, primarily English-speaking, ethnic groups surrounded them at an accelerating rate during the 1830s and 1840s. By the time the colonists from Glarus tramped through Lafayette County in 1845, the earlier Swiss had intermarried and virtually disappeared in the social warp and woof of Wisconsin Territory.

EARLIEST SWISS SETTLEMENTS

At least one partly cohesive settlement, however, did antedate New Glarus in Wisconsin. By the early 1840s several Swiss families were farming in the town of Honey Creek and elsewhere in Sauk County, which soon became heavily German in its ethnic composition. The account of these families is perhaps most lucidly, if somewhat atypically, exemplified by the saga of the Ragaz (later spelled Ragatz) clan. Its patriarch,

Bartholomäus (in America, Bartholomew) Ragaz, was the elected local and district magistrate and owned a relatively prosperous construction and lumber milling business in Tamins, a Rhenish village in the rugged southeastern canton of Graubünden. In spite of his standing in the community, he saw little prospect for the nine children of his two marriages, and he expressed pessimism about the future of Switzerland.

In 1841 he dispatched his oldest son, twenty-four-year-old Christian, to the United States to seek a suitable home for the family. The young man soon reported that the region around Galena, Illinois, bore a resemblance to Switzerland and enthusiastically encouraged the rest of the family to follow in his wake. After selling many of their possessions and completing extensive preparations for the journey, the remaining Ragazes left Tamins in March 1842, probably hoping to join Christian in time to farm with him that summer.

They traveled overland through Switzerland, the southwestern German principalities, and France and sailed from Le Havre, France, with approximately 120 other passengers and crew members on a three-masted vessel commanded by an inexperienced American mariner. After a marathon crossing of sixty-one days marked by several unpleasant and dangerous episodes, the polyglot immigrants disembarked at New Orleans in late June.

They continued aboard a Mississippi River steamboat to St. Louis, where the Ragazes parted company with their fellow passengers and continued on to Galena, only to discover that Christian had accepted a job supervising construction in the infant Wisconsin River village of Sauk City. Equipped with two horse carts, the family set out for Sauk County and were reunited with the young man three days later. The Ragazes soon staked a claim of no fewer than 640 acres in nearby Honey Creek Township, but they lived in Christian's cabin the first winter. The elder Ragaz retained, unofficially, his title of magistrate and was repeatedly asked to mediate controversies among settlers who had known him in Graubünden.

Members of at least three other families from Switzerland also arrived at Sauk City in 1842. This nucleus attracted considerable migration to Sauk County before the middle of the nineteenth century. Some came perhaps in response to Bartholomew Ragaz's glowing reports published in the cantonal newspapers. Others were prompted to leave the canton of Graubünden in 1842 when an avalanche destroyed part of Felsberg, a dorp near Tamins. Many of its dispossessed residents packed their personal effects and relocated in Sauk County. Forty-one families reportedly arrived in the summer of 1843. Donations collected throughout much of Switzerland defrayed part of the cost of their passage. Although by 1847 one of the Graubünden expatriates was able to write home from Sauk Prairie that some fifty families from there dominated the region, other parts of the confederation also contributed to the peopling of southern Wisconsin. John Bosshard, a native of Nänikon, immigrated to New York in 1844 and resettled in Sauk County in either 1847 or 1848. He encouraged many of his fellow Nänikonites to join him there in the late 1840s and early 1850s.

Swiss immigrants also settled elsewhere in Wisconsin before 1850, though only in small numbers. By 1847 Buffalo County, which eventually had one of the largest Swiss populations in the state, included a few who had previously lived in Galena. At approximately the same time, natives of the northeastern canton of St. Gallen began to farm in Fond du Lac County. Not all of the early Swiss in Wisconsin hailed from the German-speaking cantons, however. In 1848 Maurice Deléglise, a native of Valais, emigrated to the "pretty village" of Theresa in Dodge County and bought a forty-acre farm not far from several other francophone former residents of Valais, who had already settled there. During the next few years some of Deléglise's relatives joined him.

SWISS SETTLEMENT PATTERNS

Owing primarily to the settlements in Green and Sauk counties, Wisconsin boasted 1,224 of the nation's 13,358 Swiss immigrants in 1850. The state ranked fourth behind Ohio (which led with 3,291 Swiss-born residents), New York, and Illinois. Nevertheless, those 1,224 Helvetians were but a small chip in the kaleidoscope of Wisconsin's ethnicity. The state already numbered more than 40,000 German immigrants (its largest ethnic group from continental Europe), 21,043 newcomers from Ireland, 18,952 from England, 8,651 Norwegians, and 8,277 Canadians. On the other hand, the Swiss outnumbered the French, the Netherlanders, the Belgians, the Danes, the Austrians, and the Russians in Wisconsin at mid-century. The migration of most of these groups, all of which have played significant roles in the state's history, was still in its infancy. The same was true of the Swiss.

Throughout the nineteenth century and into the twentieth, Wisconsin maintained a high ranking in its number of Swiss-born residents. By 1870 it had dropped into fifth place behind Ohio, New York, Illinois, and Missouri. Twenty years later Wisconsin's total had climbed to 7,181, reaching 7,666 at the turn of the century and cresting at 8,036 in 1910, despite the deaths of many early settlers and the removal of others to southern Minnesota as well as other states and territories. At no census up to and including that of 1930, when mass European immigration was a phenomenon of the past, did Wisconsin rank lower than sixth in the nation in its number of Swiss residents, and usually it occupied fifth place. Equally significant, all of the states with larger absolute numbers of Swiss-born residents had far greater populations. On a percentage basis, therefore, Wisconsin is arguably the most Swiss state in the Union, even though in both absolute and relative terms its citizens tracing their roots to Switzerland have always been overshadowed by Germans, Irish, Norwegians, and other ethnic groups.

The settlement pattern of the Swiss in Wisconsin reveals much about their occupational life and possibly something of their relations with other ethnic groups. When the 1880s, the peak decade for Swiss migration, drew to a close, the vast majority resided in the state's two southernmost tiers of counties. Green County numbered no fewer than 1,866 Swiss-born residents, or 26 percent of the total. Nearly all of these lived in Monroe or the steadily growing New Glarus settlement. But for all the attention historians and others have given the latter, most of Wisconsin's Swiss in 1890 obviously were elsewhere. Owing partly to migration from New Glarus, the adjacent counties of Dane, Rock, and Lafayette had substantial numbers, most of whom were still engaged in agriculture. Farther afield, Buffalo County on the Mississippi River had 680 in 1890, far and away the largest concentration in western Wisconsin. La Crosse County numbered 294 first-generation Swiss Americans, and Sauk County 346.

It is interesting to note that in all of these counties and several others with concentrations of Swiss immigrants the Germans were the dominant foreign-born group. To be sure, Germans were the largest immigrant community at that time in nearly the entire state, including many areas that never attracted more than a handful of Swiss settlers. It is also true that the Swiss were conspicuously absent from those areas where few Germans had settled, such as ethnically heterogeneous Douglas Counny, heavily Swedish Burnett County, or the Norwegian bastion of Vernon County. Some kind of correlation seems evident. It is difficult to demonstrate precisely why the Swiss often followed in the footprints of German immigrants, but it seems plausible that language played a certain role, especially if Swiss newcomers learned of recently settled areas through the German American press. Most of Wisconsin's immigrants from Switzerland were natives of its German-speaking cantons, and their aversion to the "German" label was not necessarily great during the nineteenth century.

In contrast to their concentrations in such cities as St. Louis, Cincinnati, New York, San Francisco, and Paterson, New Jersey, the Swiss of Wisconsin long remained overwhelmingly rural. In 1870 only 346, or 5.7 percent, resided in Milwaukee, where they were vastly outnumbered (and no doubt in many cases culturally engulfed) by the city's more than 20,000 Germans. As the industrialization of Wisconsin continued during the 1890s and the early twentieth century, significant though hardly profound changes in the distribution of the state's Swiss indicate a moderate urbanization.

The city of Milwaukee had 584 Swiss-born residents in 1890, 653 in 1900, and 833 in 1910, an increase of nearly 43 percent in two decades. The figure climbed to 1,137 (713 of them men) in 1930. By then 2,810 of the state's first-generation Swiss Americans were classified as urban and 4,859 as rural. (For purposes of comparison, about 63 percent of Wisconsin's German immigrants were officially urban in 1930, but only 38.2 percent of the Norwegians and 36.6 percent of the Swiss were urban.) In short, the strong majority of those who came from Switzerland settled and remained on farms or in small towns. It was largely their children, and not the immigrants themselves, who participated in post–World War I migration from rural areas to Milwaukee and other cities.

WHO WERE THE EMIGRATING SWISS?

Why did these and approximately 400,000 other Swiss leave their native country? From a post–World War II perspective, when Switzerland had attained unprecedented — and almost unparalleled — prosperity and indeed attracted an alien population numbering several hundred thousand, which, by 2005, had grown to more than one and a half million, it is difficult to visualize the poverty and other burdens that once prompted an exodus from that Alpine land. During the nineteenth century and the early years of the twentieth, however, Switzerland shared many of the hardships that hampered most other European economies.

Actually, emigration from Switzerland to America began much earlier. Before the United States came into being, more than 20,000 Swiss had settled in the English colonies. Religious and political persecution, personal problems, economic woes, and other factors had compelled them to opt for a new start in the relatively primitive surroundings of North America. Pennsylvania and New York attracted considerable numbers, but place-names such as New Bern, North Carolina, testify to their presence in the southern colonies as well.

After 1800 the population explosion and Industrial Revolution, which eventually transformed most of Europe, left a deep stamp on Switzerland. The Swiss did not multiply as rapidly as the Scandinavians, for instance, but even an undramatic increase in their numbers strained the country's resources. In 1837 Switzerland had a population of slightly fewer than 2,200,000. This rose to more than 3,300,000 by the end of the century and to 3,880,000 in 1920. At the same time, the Industrial Revolution changed what had been a predominantly rural society into one with an urban sector of considerable dimensions. Geneva, a quiet town of 22,000 in 1800, had become a bustling if sedate city of 59,000 a century later. More dramatically, Zurich waxed from 12,000 to 151,000 during the same period. Much of the cities' growth was the result of influx from the countryside, which could not support the excess population that a decreasing death rate (especially a decline in infant mortality owing to advances in health care) had bestowed on it.

Curiously, however, nineteenth-century Switzerland attracted people from foreign countries while losing many of its own to them. When Swiss emigration crested in the 1880s, the country accommodated more than two hundred thousand aliens, nearly half of them Germans and the remainder French and Italians. These foreigners, largely unskilled laborers, took industrial and construction jobs that dispossessed rural Swiss bypassed on their road to inexpensive or free farmland overseas.

Most emigrating Swiss found new homes in North America, but large numbers remained in Europe and settled in France, Germany, and Italy. For those who left the continent, Latin America provided alternatives to the United States; in 1880 Argentina had more than 12,000 Swiss-born residents and Brazil more than 2,200. Australia then numbered some 2,300 and Algeria 3,000. Nevertheless, the United States already led with 88,621 of the nearly quarter-million Swiss abroad at that time, and its proportion increased notably during the next thirty years. Between 1887 and 1938 no less than 73 percent of emigrating Swiss landed in the United States. (Argentina ranked second, receiving a little over 10 percent.)

Most of the Swiss cantons lost sizable portions of their residents to emigration, though some gave up far more than others. In absolute terms, the Protestant, German-speaking cantons of Bern and Zurich lost the most, though on a per capita basis they ranked ninth and seventh, respectively, during the late nineteenth and early twentieth centuries. The Italianate canton of Ticino suffered the greatest relative loss and the third largest numerically between 1887 and 1938. Generally speaking, the francophone cantons of western Switzerland retained greater percentages of their populations than did other regions. Consequently, the speakers of German dialects, who now constitute more than 63 percent of the Swiss citizenry, were represented to an even greater degree among Swiss Americans, including those in Wisconsin.

Although it is nearly impossible to limn an analytical profile of those who settled in the Badger State, much is known about the characteristics of emigrating Swiss generally, especially those who left after 1880. Like that from many other European countries, the migration from Switzerland was disproportionately one of young adults. Only about 17 percent of the Swiss were then in their twenties, but more than 40 percent of those who departed were in that age group. Teenagers were also strongly represented in the emigration, as were people in their thirties. Middle-aged and especially older Swiss understandably tended to forgo the rigors of resettling abroad. More than 70 percent were unmarried. Of those with occupational designations, a third had been involved in agriculture, which then employed about 25 percent of the Swiss population. Artisans whose skills had been rendered obsolete by machines also emigrated in relatively large numbers. Otherwise, the migration spanned a broad selection of occupations.

Such factors as fluctuations in the American economy helped determine the flow from Switzerland to the United States. Prospective emigrants were often relatively well informed about the possibility of employment in the New World, and they postponed their departures when those chances seemed remote. The prosperous 1850s — at least before the Panic of 1857 — were thus a period of heavy immigration, the first such decade for the Swiss. Probably because of the Civil War, there was a decline in the 1860s, and there was only a moderate rise during the decade following the depression of 1873. In the 1880s, however, the number of Swiss arriving in the United States nearly trebled to more than 80,000. The peak year was 1883 with approximately 13,500. The flow tapered off during the economically troubled 1890s but surged again on a smaller scale after the turn of the century.

The government of Wisconsin did not wait passively for the American economy to draw Swiss and other European immigrants to the Midwest. Shortly after the middle of the nineteenth century, it began to recruit settlers actively through advertisements in European newspapers, roseate descriptions of the state in pamphlets published in several languages, and an agent stationed in New York City. Such activities, the first by any Midwestern state, were expanded in 1853, but the following year anti-immigrant sentiment was rife in Wisconsin, and the legislature eliminated the New York office. During its brief existence it aimed much of its efforts at German-speaking immigrants and no doubt thereby contacted many of Swiss origin.

When the influx into America rose to new heights after the Civil War, Wisconsin resumed its efforts to recruit European newcomers, largely through a Board of Immigration founded in 1867 that competed with similar agencies representing other states. On occasion it also funded local agents who assisted immigrants in Milwaukee and Chicago. The board struggled financially for several years, and it is difficult to gauge how instrumental it was in convincing immigrants from Switzerland and elsewhere in Europe to opt for Wisconsin. Because it invested much of its limited funds in German publications, however, it seems most plausible that the board played a contributing role in attracting Swiss newcomers.

Unofficially, Swiss already in Wisconsin often urged compatriots to join them, while real estate agencies and others with vested interests in promoting Wisconsin also helped attract Helvetian immigrants to the state.

CROSSING THE ATLANTIC

The Atlantic crossing was one of the few common denominators among European immigrants. It temporarily cast together polyglot peoples, many of whom had long traditions of hostility with one another. On board immigrant ships, new kinds of tension and struggles often erupted. Passengers occasionally fought for their lives against the rages of epidemics and, in the early days, often lost. Tempers frequently flared in cramped quarters. Charges of mistreatment and exploitation by crew members were not uncommon. On the whole, the Atlantic crossing was a disharmonic prelude to the challenges that immigrants faced in the New World. But even among a relatively small ethnic group like the Swiss, conditions of the voyage differed immensely.

From landlocked Switzerland there was no natural continental point of embarkation. Le Havre, reached by rail via Paris, was a favorite, as were Antwerp, Belgium; and Bremen and Hamburg, Germany. Many chose a more complicated if sometimes less expensive route involving overland travel to the English Channel, a ferry crossing to Britain, and a rail journey to Liverpool, where they joined multilingual hordes awaiting departure on British or other steamships.

Those who emigrated before the Civil War often sailed on American vessels. As steam power gradually replaced sails during the 1860s and 1870s, large German and British lines captured the lion's share of the immigrant traffic. Heavy competition among these behemoths drove prices down, although they fluctuated as the flow of migrants waxed and waned. When relatively few Europeans were making the crossing, the shipping companies discounted their fares to attract at least a moderate number of passengers and thereby cut the losses incurred in making scheduled crossings. At such times tickets, often prepaid by relatives and friends already in America, were modestly priced but nonetheless could entail several months' wages.

Swiss passengers, like emigrants from most other European countries, wrote countless letters home decrying conditions on board. One fairly affluent family that sailed from Le Havre in 1842 was fortunate enough to book cabin fares for approximately twenty dollars per person on an American vessel. Their quarters were cramped and, according to one of the sons, "When we got to the tropics and it grew hot, the older boys took their mattresses out on deck and slept under the stars, but I never did." Instead, the venturesome youth explored the conditions that less-privileged emigrants endured in steerage. "The other passengers all slept in one enormous room below, each family between its own trunks," he recalled. "There was straw and sawdust on the floor down there. We children often went down to visit new friends until mother found vermin on us." After two eventful months at sea they finally disembarked in New Orleans. More typically, however, sailing ships made the crossing in six or seven weeks and docked at East Coast ports.

The advent of steam power on the North Atlantic shipping lanes slashed this marathon to a comparative sprint of ten or twelve days. Shipboard outbreaks of cholera, smallpox, and typhus became largely nightmares of the past, though before the enactment of stricter maritime legislation in the twentieth century, conditions remained putrid for passengers in steerage. Paul Brandt, a Swiss journalist, offered a description of the infernal environment after his journey to America in 1893: "Whoever opens his eyes and does not have particularly weak nerves can here study how the working class scrimps, struggles, suffers, and endures. Here is the pale, haggard, sickly mother nursing her screaming infant while supporting her throbbing head in her thin hand. There is the colorless father with a small boy and a somewhat larger girl on his chest. Here are two sisters, huddled together, and there a shaking old woman fearfully watching over her slumbering grandchild."

AGRICULTURE, OLD WORLD AND NEW

Despite the fact that agriculture formed the backbone of Switzerland's economy throughout the nineteenth century, Swiss immigrants in Wisconsin had to adapt to American ways of farming. Helvetian farms were universally small, indeed minute compared to those in the United States, and typically they encompassed only a few hectares. Moreover, in most instances the convoluted holdings of the Swiss farmers were only partly tillable, and much of them were used for hay to feed cattle. Potatoes were a common crop, while small grains played a minor role in the agriculture of Switzerland. In short, the cultivation of large acreages so common in North America was simply impossible in Switzerland, where plots were long worked with spades rather than plows and families used rakes to gather their hay until well into the twentieth century.

Being unfamiliar with the size of American farms, the Emigration Society of Glarus had optimistically aimed to settle families on twenty-acre plots. On their way down the Ohio River, however, Dürst and Streiff learned that such acreages were only marginally viable. But, limited by the funds at their disposal, they could not purchase larger farms.

Consequently, one of the first priorities of the settlers at New Glarus was to acquire additional land, a goal largely achieved by 1860, when their 149 farms totaled more than ten thousand acres.

Twenty years later, when many members of the second generation had also become farmers and the settlement had attracted later immigrants, more than sixty thousand acres of the area's agricultural land was in Swiss hands.

Plowing virgin land was a new experience to these newcomers. Many of them had never used a plow in the old country, where plots had been cultivated with little interruption for generations. The new implement naturally required a team of horses or a yoke of oxen, either of which involved a considerable outlay of cash. In New Glarus, where cash initially was in short supply, the settlers purchased collectively four yoke of oxen the year after their arrival and used the overworked beasts in rotation to break their land.

Bartholomew Ragatz, whose family had more capital than most and whose full-section (640-acre) farm in Sauk County dwarfed the acreages of most newcomers, acquired twelve oxen in less than two years and earned a large profit doing custom plowing for other farmers at the then rather steep rate of $2.25 to $2.75 per acre. His son Oswald, not yet a teenager, had the chore of navigating approximately seven tons of beef through the fields while Oswald's older brother John Henry manned the thirty-inch breaker plow. "Handling this number of oxen is no light task," Oswald recalled, "and I got plenty of lung exercise shouting at the stolid creatures." Complicating matters, "the grass and underbrush often came up to my shoulders as I trudged alongside the oxen. The roots clung tenaciously to the soil and every inch was a hard pull — often a struggle. But furrow by furrow we triumphed over the wilderness."

The first crops were naturally labor-intensive ones, which required relatively little land and could be consumed locally. The settlers at New Glarus at first emphasized beans, potatoes, pumpkins, and tobacco. As more land was cleared, they planted increasing amounts of small grain. Wheat was especially popular and at times brought considerable profits, as in 1854 when it fetched more than a dollar a bushel. Chinch bugs reduced yields some years, however, and inadequate soil conservation took its toll. Characteristic of subsistence farmers, the Swiss kept large vegetable gardens, which continued to supply much of their nourishment long after the immigrants began to sell their produce for cash.

Nature supplemented their diets. "Deer, rabbits, squirrels, and prairie chickens abounded," wrote one early arrival. "Likewise, there were passenger pigeons which flew in such numbers that we could see them pass overhead in long lines for hours at a time. We shot and snared them by the hundred, and mother cooked them and packed them away in jars of lard for future use." The numerous streams yielded large catches of fish that brought an additional measure of nutritional variety to the settlers' rough-hewn tables. Nevertheless, the fare could be monotonous for those not yet established on productive farmsteads. One who arrived at New Glarus in 1850 wrote home dejectedly that he ate boiled potatoes three times a day.

As the immigrants acquired more cash and land, their holdings of livestock expanded quite rapidly. Statistics kept at New Glarus vividly reveal this waxing prosperity. According to admittedly unreliable records, the number of cattle on its farms climbed from 94 in 1846 to 182 in 1849. More markedly, the swine population escalated from 193 to 1,482 during the same three-year period. Similar growth rates characterized Swiss farms elsewhere in Wisconsin. One of the Ragatz brothers remembered: "After the first year [when a severe winter blizzard killed all of their sheep, nine of their cattle, an unspecified number of pigs, and nearly claimed Bartholomew's life] we always had beef and pork — fresh, salted, pickled, or smoked — in great quantity [and] chicken was a regular article of diet."

With their expanding herds of cattle, the immigrants began dairy farming quite early. This was one of the few branches of agriculture in which they could transplant Old World expertise directly to the New, and the Swiss merit considerable credit for transforming Wisconsin into "America's Dairyland." In addition to producing milk, they helped to establish the important cheese industry in the southern region of the state. Part of the production naturally was Swiss cheese of the familiar Emmentaler variety that farmers began to make shortly after arriving in America. But not all were familiar with production methods. Bartholomew Ragatz, for instance, had to learn the technique from a book while his wife made butter in their four-room cabin.

Commercial production of cheese in Green County began in 1869 in Washington Township. A decade later, lawyer John Luchsinger of Monroe, who had settled in New Glarus in 1856, lamented that the quality of the area's Swiss cheese had already begun to decline. Far more of the commodity, however (three-quarters, according to Luchsinger), was of the more profitable and pungent Limburger type, whose roots can be traced to Belgium. The Swiss American attorney boasted that much of the 300 tons made annually was shipped to domestic markets or exported to Britain and, incredibly, to Switzerland. In 1873 the first cheese factory, an enterprise that specialized in American cheese, was built in the village of New Glarus.

The immigrants' cattle may not have shared their owners' enthusiasm for the dairy business. Many of the newcomers justifiably found Midwestern winters more severe than those of Switzerland. Exacerbating matters, as a farmer near Sauk Prairie wrote to his brother in Graubünden, "There are only low hills between which the north wind blows very strongly." Nevertheless, he reported, "not all of the cattle are stabled. As a result, they are a sad sight by spring." He consoled himself that "during the summer time they are as well off as those in Europe."

In the consumption of wine the Swiss rank among the leading European nations, so it was natural for those who emigrated to undertake viticulture in America. One who settled in Honey Creek Township near Sauk Prairie in 1847 brought with him from Switzerland a number of vine cuttings, which he optimistically transplanted in Wisconsin soil. To his dismay, they failed to survive the first winter. He wrote home pessimistically that only imported grape seeds would germinate in the area. Although his brother-in-law sent him a package of seeds from Switzerland, he apparently did not participate in any noteworthy way in the largely German attempts to develop a wine industry in Sauk County during the 1840s. The same entrepreneur found countless wild grapevines in the hills, which regrettably proved unsuitable for profitable wine mak-ing. The saving grace of the grapes, he remarked, was that they "have such a strongly colored juice that one can write letters with it."

The Ragatz clan planted vine cuttings sent from Switzerland, but the quality of the grapes was disappointing. The family made grape and el-derberry wine from the fruits of nature, however, and fashioned wooden casks and a press from local materials. One of the sons described the results of their efforts as "excellent." Further quenching their thirst, the Ragatzes cultivated hops and brewed their own beer.

Many Swiss farmers in southwestern Wisconsin supplemented their initially meager incomes through outside employment. Only a minority of the immigrants had been engaged in agriculture in their homeland; their ranks included men whose backgrounds covered a fairly broad spec-trum of other pursuits. The pioneers at New Glarus, for instance, had worked as carpenters, printers, coopers, lumberjacks, slaters, handymen, and — reflecting Swiss tradition at its worst — mercenaries. Some of their expertise was in demand on the Wisconsin frontier and in northern Illinois. Other Swiss accepted positions as unskilled laborers to tide them and their families over until their new homesteads became large and pro-ductive enough to furnish adequate support.

In the early years the womenfolk shared the burden of supplemen-tary labor. Well accustomed to physical work in Switzerland, many of them augmented their families' incomes by toiling as washerwomen, as maids, and in other capacities for paltry wages. Nor did their husbands earn princely remuneration as hired hands on the farms of earlier set-tlers; the typical wage for such work was about half a dollar per day, often paid *in natura*. A few months after arriving at Sauk Prairie in 1847, Jakob Bühler, a carpenter by training, and two colleagues spent several days dig-ging potatoes and received about eight bushels of the tubers for their backbreaking efforts.

The relative prosperity of the early 1850s, however, brought greater compensation for such agricultural labor. Bühler's younger brother Ulrich boasted of being worth up to eighteen dollars a month as a hired hand. The youth confessed to a friend in Switzerland that he had previ-ously commanded a mere third of that wage. But setting his sights higher still, the ambitious young Bühler considered hiring on as a lumberjack at no less than twenty dollars a month.

In posed testimony to the popularity of target shooting among men and women, these three Swiss women were photographed with what they called their "schuetzen-rifles" by Gerhard Gesell in his Alma studio around the turn of the century.

WHi Image ID 9831

WHi Image ID 42745

Governor Emanuel Philipp and his herd on his Sauk County farm

WHi Image ID 27421

Above: A stereoview of New Glarus by Andrew Dahl taken about 1873–1879. The larger, towered church in the background is the Swiss (Zwingli) Reformed Church.

Right: Reverend Oswald Ragatz.

WHi Image ID 42741

Left: Reverend Wilhelm Streissguth.

Below: The Jacob Gasser family stand in front of their Tower Rock Farm near Prairie du Sac in 1898.

WHi Image ID 40206

This 1928 photo records the enduring craftsmanship of a Swiss woodworker about 1853 in Monroe.

WHi Image ID 42742

The vinegar factory of Benedict Goldenberger, who came to Madison in 1857.

WHi Image ID 1971

Goldenberger descendants at a wurst roast in the Madison vicinity about 1913.

WHi Image ID 25660

Abraham Schmoker and kitten enjoy the sunshine in front of Schmoker's home. Schmoker left his native Switzerland and settled at Holmes Landing (Fountain City) in Buffalo County in 1849.

The Alma law office of Theodore Buehler Sr., whose father had emigrated from Switzerland in 1850, eventually arriving at Holmes Landing (Fountain City) in 1852.

SERVICE IN THE CIVIL WAR

When the guns of April ignited the Civil War in 1861, many first- and second-generation Swiss in Wisconsin echoed the rhetoric of martial hysteria then prevalent and joined in the carnage, which eventually cost more American lives than World Wars I and II combined. In New Glarus, which had a tradition of gun clubs, the fever seems to have been especially intense. A disenchanted observer in nearby Dayton wrote in October 1861 that an irregular company in New Glarus included forty-six volunteers who trained daily. The following month the *Sentinel* in Monroe reported that several dozen armed men from the neighboring township had marched through the community on their way to assignment. Eventually nearly 100 New Glarus men stood under arms. Many served in the Second and Ninth Wisconsin Volunteer Infantry Regiments, while others were assigned to several different outfits. They participated in bloody combat at Gettysburg, at Antietam, and on battlefields elsewhere, inevitably suffering their share of casualties while reportedly inflicting still more. Perhaps they dispatched some of their erstwhile compatriots who had settled in the South and were fighting under the colors of the Confederate forces, thus unwittingly bringing to American shores oblique reverberations of the intercantonal strife that had occasionally stained the history of Switzerland.

Not all of these warriors spoke or understood English, one factor that no doubt impeded their comprehension of the issues involved. Their motives for signing up may well have included a thirst for adventure and violence, a susceptibility to group pressure, the inability to envisage non-violent means of resolving conflicts, and so forth; but in wartime correspondence they professed high-mindedness to justify their role in the carnage. Gottfried Bosshard, for example, marched off to war in 1861 assuring his parents and brother that "the matter was too holy for me to be held back by difficulties." Acknowledging the risk involved, he professed that if he were killed in action his family would at least have the consolation of knowing that he had given his life for a "holy cause." On the other hand, young Bosshard reasoned, if he returned alive he would have a lot to tell them and would have done something useful.

From a hospital bed at Fort Leavenworth, Kansas, he revealed six-

teen months later that his fervor had not diminished. The draft riots of
1863, in which immigrants and Native Americans alike protested against
military conscription, particularly irked Bosshard. It was the duty of
every able-bodied young man to support the Constitution and the main-
tenance of law, he insisted. The incipient protest movement was therefore "treason," which hurt the Union's military efforts more than
Confederate attacks could. Bosshard vowed "not to return home until the
Stars and Stripes again flies over the territory of the United States as it
had before the outbreak of the war." Meanwhile, Swiss Americans found
themselves apologizing to relatives in Switzerland for the younger generation's militancy. Maurice Deléglise, the man from Valais who had fought
for the autonomy of several Catholic cantons in the Swiss civil war of
1847, defended his son's participation in that of the United States. "You
tell me that Augustin would have done better to remain here instead
of going to war," he wrote to a cousin in 1863, "but what about me? If I
had not gone to the war of the *Sonderbund*, would you have esteemed me
as a good citizen?" Repeating familiar sentiments of the day, the elder
Deléglise declared that "to fight for emancipation from slavery is the
greatest act of charity that a man can perform."

He understood that philanthropy of the armed sort did not come
cheaply. His son had received three wounds in Maryland the previous
year, but despite the decimation of his company, he had returned to active duty after recovering. Young Deléglise was nearly killed at Gettysburg
in July of 1863, and he was wounded yet again, though less seriously,
early the following year.

THE POLITICAL ARENA

If many Swiss immigrants zealously plunged into the Civil War, they generally showed more restraint in entering the political arena of their new
homeland. Their cautious involvement is perhaps best understood
against the backdrop of nineteenth-century constitutional developments
in Switzerland, which pitched and rolled through troubled waters on its
voyage toward the achievement of democratic ideals.

The political history of the Swiss confederation, which dates from
the thirteenth century, entered a new phase as Napoleon's armies prop-

agated throughout much of Europe the upheavals wrought by the French Revolution. The advent of French troops in Switzerland in 1797 and 1798 prompted several cantons to widen their narrowly defined franchise and led to the establishment of the unitary Helvetian Republic in the latter year.

Under the aegis of France, the Helvetian constitution abolished venerable class distinctions, ensured freedom of worship and conscience, granted all citizens equality before the law, and established an indirectly elected government based largely on French models. Napoleon's Mediation Constitution of 1803 liberated the Swiss peasantry from its feudal obligations, supported popular education, separated church and state, bestowed citizenship on additional Swiss, and moved the country closer to the ideal of *égalité*.

The defeat of Napoleon and the restoration of the conservative order in many European countries also had repercussions in Switzerland. A reactionary constitution ratified in 1815 superseded that of 1803. It reversed some reforms but guaranteed limited democracy in the majority of the cantons while cementing the domination of the upper class and the guilds in others.

As in several other countries, however, much of the post-Napoleonic generation in Switzerland clamored for greater freedom of expression, religious toleration, and other rights, especially after the July Revolution of 1830 brought the ostensibly reform-minded Louis Philippe to the French throne. Swiss conservatives, though, especially in the Catholic cantons, resisted further reforms and the greater degree of centralization through which they were to be effected. The brief *Sonderbund* war of 1847 ended in the defeat of an alliance of the insurgent Catholic cantons and the reassertion of the fundamental unity of the country at the expense of cantonal sovereignty. A constitution adopted in 1848 guaranteed many of the freedoms that still obtain in Switzerland today. Political parties then began to play an important role in Swiss politics.

Emerging from this cauldron of democracy in the making, the Swiss of Wisconsin might have been expected to take an active part in the political life of their new land. But initially few seem to have done so. To some extent this can naturally be attributed to the language barrier and the fact that many Swiss did not acquire American citizenship as soon as they could have — itself an interesting phenomenon. Yet their letters to Switzerland suggest that many Swiss Americans were less interested in both local and national political developments than were, for instance, contemporary Scandinavian newcomers in Wisconsin.

Those who did become involved tended in the early decades to support the Democratic Party, probably seeing in it a parallel to the anti-patrician agrarian movements in which many had participated in Switzerland. One of Green County's first Swiss Republicans recalled that he and fewer than ten others in New Glarus had voted for Abraham Lincoln in 1860. But the Civil War, he declared, brought about a genuine duality in party loyalties, supposedly transforming "nearly all of the boys who enlisted into Republicans." As late as 1879, however, he lamented that Democratic candidates still garnered two-thirds of the Swiss vote in the area. Populism and other third-party movements had never enjoyed support among the Wisconsin Swiss, he wrote in 1894, when, presumably to the surprise of no one familiar with Swiss social life, he boasted that "there was never a Prohibitionist vote cast at all in New Glarus."

The absence of keen interest in politics did not mean apathy or antipathy toward civic life, however, and in some areas Swiss immigrants were quietly elected to public office at relatively early dates. In their bastion of Green County, the proper functioning of the community necessitated participation in local government. Shopkeeper J. J. Tschudy of New Glarus became in 1858 the first Swiss elected to county office there, serving sequentially as recorder, register, and county clerk. Others soon followed, and by the 1860s Swiss leadership on the local level was no longer a novelty. During the following decade John Luchsinger became the first Swiss to represent Green County in the state legislature. By the end of the century, several sons of immigrants from Switzerland had been sent to Madison from Green County as well as more ethnically heterogeneous districts.

No second-generation Swiss American gained more prominence in Wisconsin politics than Emanuel Lorenz Philipp. Born in a log cabin in Sauk County in 1861 to a farming couple from Graubünden, he acquired his limited formal education in the area and while still a teenager was licensed to teach. After three years in that profession, Philipp learned telegraphy and became a railway station agent in Baraboo. Later he served as a traffic manager for the Schlitz brewery, and early in the 1890s he entered the lumber business in northern Mississippi. By 1897 Philipp had returned and had become president of the Union Refrigerator Transit Company of Wisconsin.

Shortly before the turn of the century, the meteoric capitalist's interests expanded to include politics as well as business. In 1900 he was elected chairman of the Republican Party in Milwaukee County and supported Robert M. La Follette in the first of his three successful bids for the governorship, but the two Republicans soon fell out with each other. The more conservative Philipp began to oppose not only the governor's rhetoric but also several of the reforms that "Fighting Bob" and his allies were championing.

Philipp articulately presented the conservative case against direct primary elections, certain aspects of railroad regulation, and progressive taxation in *Political Reform in Wisconsin*, a book he published in 1910. He insisted that the Stalwart Republican position proceeded not from economic self-interest but from a concern for governmental frugality and a desire to foster moderate reforms in a manner less demagogic than that which La Follette frequently displayed.

Elected to the governorship in 1915, Philipp served for six years during a period of national crisis and international conflict that caused tensions in and among several of Wisconsin's largest ethnic groups. Initially isolationist, he eventually supported Woodrow Wilson's reluctant intervention in World War I and insisted on the enforcement of the conscription law. To his admirers, Philipp typified many traits of his conservative Swiss-American background.

Some natives of Switzerland translated the nineteenth-century political struggles of that country into radical politics in the United States. C. Hermann Boppe was the most prominent in Wisconsin. Born in the canton of Zug in 1842, he emigrated as a teenager and worked briefly at a brewery in New Jersey before assuming the editorship of the *Newark Post*, a progressive German-language daily. Boppe resettled in Milwaukee in 1877 and from 1879 to 1899 was at the helm of the city's radical newspaper, *Freidenker* (Freethinker). Though politically independent, he wrote and spoke incessantly about the issues of the Gilded Age.

Boppe maintained a keen interest in his native language and helped found the German-American Teachers' Seminary of Milwaukee to educate bilingual students for teaching positions in schools where either language was the medium of instruction. A nervous breakdown cut short his career in 1898, a year before his death, but by then Boppe had gained a firm reputation as a leading journalist and cultural figure in radical immigrant circles. (His activities underscore the many ties between Swiss and German newcomers in Wisconsin.)

ETHNIC RELATIONS

The history of most immigrant communities in the United States entails above all else their relations with the other ethnic groups with whom they interacted. The Swiss who settled in Wisconsin came from a land where discord among linguistic factions had multiplied tensions between Protestants and Catholics. Compounding matters, occasionally they had been at odds with the surrounding countries whose languages they shared. Finally, cantonal loyalties had roots several centuries deep, and at least some Swiss resisted the notion of a unified — or unifying — nation-state. They thus brought to American shores a curious amalgam of ethnic antipathies and affinities that often influenced their behavior in Wisconsin and their perceptions of life in the New World.

The Swiss naturally had extensive contacts with Yankees and members of other European immigrant groups. By the 1840s much of Wisconsin was ethnically pluralistic, and even in such strongholds as Green and Sauk counties the Swiss, from an early date, intermingled frequently with several other peoples. Prosperity demanded cordial relations with the English-speaking majority, which dominated commercial and political life. In New Glarus, the newcomers enjoyed the assistance of Americans who had preceded them to the vicinity and ameliorated their needs by donating a sizable quantity of provisions in 1847. "Know-Nothing" sympathies of that time did not prevent English-speaking neighbors from welcoming these strangers in their midst and offering them employment. In letters to the old country, the Swiss insisted that "the Americans" not only tolerated but even admired them. One farmer in Dane County explained in 1851 that "the Yankees regard us as excellent neighbors and tell me that they prefer us to the Irish who have begun to enter the area." An apparently Protestant mechanic in Milwaukee echoed this sentiment two years later, generalizing that, in the eyes of "the Americans," the religious beliefs of newcomers seemed to count more than their national origin.

Later in the century, as the nativist campaign to halt immigration mounted, the Swiss joined other newcomers in complaining that a xenophobic pall hung over life in some quarters. This was especially the case after 1880. On the other hand, Yankees clamoring for a reduction of the flow from abroad occasionally tempered their anti-immigrant tirades by explicitly excluding certain groups from their broadsides. In some instances the Swiss were seen as an innocuous lot and were pigeonholed alongside the English, Scots, and Scandinavians as "desirable" ingredients in the American melting pot, while southern and eastern Europeans, as well as the Irish and sometimes the Germans, were rejected as unsavory ones.

The overwhelming majority of Helvetian immigrants in Wisconsin hailed from the German-speaking cantons and inevitably interacted with newcomers from the many principalities that Bismarck welded together into the Reich in 1871. Almost of necessity, the state's many German newspapers also served the Swiss as one of their major channels of information about events in the United States. This reliance, among other connections, probably augmented their sense of affinity with the much larger Teutonic group. No doubt owing to the course of modern European history as well as to their own nationalism, twentieth-century natives of Graübunden and Glarus, for instance, would stridently reject suggestions that they are "Germans." Yet their distant cousins in nineteenth- and early-twentieth-century Wisconsin were forever being identified as such, a phenomenon less natural than it may seem, because the cantonal patois of Switzerland bear relatively little resemblance to most other German dialects, save some in what is now the southwestern corner of the Federal Republic of Germany. No less surprisingly, Swiss in Wisconsin at times applied the German appellation to themselves.

THE SWIFT CURRENT OF AMERICANIZATION

Interaction with other ethnic groups inevitably contributed to assimilation, even though many Swiss immigrants sought to retain at least some aspects of their heritage. Some were partly successful, New Glarus offering an obvious if unrepresentative example. But the dispersion of the Swiss throughout much of southern Wisconsin and their relatively small numbers militated against cultural retention. Consequently, within a generation most lost much of their distinctively Swiss character, and by about 1920 little of it remained outside Green County. Though they venerated their national and cantonal heritage, the Helvetians of Wisconsin found it no less difficult than members of most other small immigrant communities to swim against a swift current of Americanization.

One of the early victims was the monolithic Swiss family. "Very rarely do the Swiss here intermarry with people of other nationalities," wrote their amateur historian John Luchsinger in 1879; "almost without exception they marry among their own country folk." His generalization arose from observations in Green County and is hardly valid for the Swiss of Wisconsin in general. The surplus men among them had no alternative but to seek non-Swiss spouses. Not surprisingly, they most frequently found them among German immigrants. The census of 1900 enumerated no fewer than 2,163 Wisconsinites born of Swiss fathers and German mothers. Among other immigrant wives in such mixed marriages, Austrian women ranked a distant second; by the turn of the century there were only sixty-nine offspring from such unions. In choosing spouses from other ethnic groups, of course, the Swiss were doing nothing unique. The phenomenon was almost inevitable among immigrants, particularly where their small numbers limited their choice of mates.

The presence of two languages in some of the resulting families naturally countered whatever efforts parents may have made to impart their own tongue to their children, thus accelerating the second generation's transition to English. But the language of the immigrants also changed. A period of linguistic transition began shortly after their arrival in America, if not before. A host of English personal and place-names augmented their German and French vocabularies, and their diction was soon filled with hitherto unknown units of measure such as bushel and acre. Newcomers' blended speech also included words that obviously had German and French counterparts but reflected in the New World objects different from those familiar in the Old. The word *fence* was an early case in point. Instead of translating it as *Zaun* when speaking or writing German, some simply borrowed the English term when referring to a distinctly American form of barrier. This amalgamation continued in the second generation as children merged their parents' tongues with that of their American playmates. In an essentially German letter of 1871, for instance, John Bosshard Jr. of Bangor listed among recent Christmas presents candy, gaiters, a whip, a diary, and a silver-plated tobacco box. All of these terms had German equivalents, as did the ladies stockings he had curiously won at a recent fair. But the proper counterparts were by then overshadowed by common English loanwords.

Education speeded the assimilation process, while newspapers both retarded and prompted it. The early settlers at New Glarus temporarily had a German-language school, but it eventually gave way to an English one. There, as at the many other schools that Swiss American children attended, the curricular materials were naturally in the official language of the United States, and lessons in history and other subjects helped form the pupils' identity as Americans. No doubt the participation of many young immigrants and the sons of immigrants in the Civil War performed a similar function.

Despite the popularity of German immigrant newspapers among the Wisconsin Swiss and the fact that they edited a few in that language, the English-language press served as a normative channel of information for most, especially in the second generation. As bilingualism ebbed among these offspring, their allegiance to such papers as the *Deutsch Schweize-rischer Courier* of New Glarus waned. Characteristic of immigrant history generally, this transition accelerated rapidly during the xenophobic days of World War I. Though foreign tongues were not banned from public use in Wisconsin as they were in Iowa, for instance, more subtle pressure served the same intolerant end to some degree. In April 1917 the editor of the *Deutsch Schweizerischer Courier*, then in its twentieth year, announced its merger with the parallel English-language *New Glarus Post*, published by the same firm. He lamented that "the younger generation is only weakly familiar with written German and does not derive the same pleasure from reading it as English." Increasing reluctance to tackle the language of their forefathers had skewed the numerical relationship between the community's two newspapers. "Especially during the last two years not a week has gone by without a subscriber switching from the German edition to the English one. . . . We have had weeks when five or more such changes were made." Presumably it was little consolation to this village journalist that the bells were simultaneously tolling for hundreds of other foreign-language newspapers in the United States, including many in Wisconsin.

RELIGIOUS LIFE

In spiritual matters, many Wisconsin Swiss upheld an approximation of their Old World heritage, probably a higher proportion than among their German counterparts in the state. Secularization came slower to

Switzerland than to many other countries; centuries-old religious loyalties and practices remained fairly firmly rooted among both Protestants of the Reformed tradition, who formed a small majority of the confederation's population, and its sizable Catholic minority. In most of the cantons either one denomination or the other was tax-supported, whereas in the United States, where more than half the population lacked formal religious affiliation, Swiss immigrants found and quickly adjusted to a fundamental separation of church and state. Partly owing to their interaction with German Americans, it is impossible to determine statistically how many of them joined any church. There is considerable evidence, however, of extensive religious activity in Swiss immigrant communities.

Due to such factors as a shortage of clergymen and the influence of other denominations, religion often assumed new forms. One of the Ragatz brothers in Sauk County recalled that in the absence of a minister, his father occasionally filled a similar role as a layman. "Father sometimes read a sermon — at other times he preached his own. . . . The difficulty was the doubt he felt with respect to his spiritual leadership." The elder Ragatz continued to deliver his homilies but refused to violate traditional clerical prerogative by administering the sacraments. Under the influence of pietistic German evangelists in the region, two of his sons eventually left the Reformed wing of Protestantism and became ministers in the rival Evangelical Association.

Perhaps nowhere was the Swiss Reformed Church more directly transplanted than to New Glarus. The size and prosperity of that colony allowed it to erect a modest log sanctuary in 1849 — four years after the first cabins went up — that housed early informal worship services. In 1850 an ordained minister, Wilhelm Streissguth, accepted a call to New Glarus with an initial salary of two hundred dollars per annum. His Reformed congregation grew and, under a different name reflecting a denominational merger with American bodies, still exists in the community. Not all of its nominal members burned with religious zeal, however. In 1896 a subsequent minister noted that "so many people, who were well and strong, had no desire to keep the Lord's day holy, so that it often happened that empty pews stared me in the face when I entered the House of the Lord. . . ."

As elsewhere, religious pluralism soon complicated the spiritual life of New Glarus. Again, the rival was the pietistic Evangelical Association. Distrusting competition, which they had not known in Switzerland, some of the Reformed stridently resisted its incursions. Consequently, when the Evangelicals won enough converts locally to form a viable congregation, they constructed their first sanctuary outside New Glarus and thus away from potential disturbances by their Reformed opponents. By 1865, however, hostile sentiments had cooled and the smaller flock relocated its house of worship in the village. The congregation eventually became part of one of the nation's largest denominations, the United Methodist Church.

Roman Catholics were decidedly a minority among Swiss immigrants in Wisconsin. Because relatively few from the Catholic cantons settled as units of any size, they were unable to form parishes with a distinctly Swiss stamp. Affiliation with parishes populated by other ethnic groups, usually German but occasionally French, thus became the norm. The Swiss have played a fairly prominent role in Catholic monasticism in the United States. An example in Wisconsin was the Capuchin friary founded in Milwaukee in 1856. That city's most visible Swiss cleric was John Martin Henni (1805–1881), an immigrant of 1828 who became its first bishop in 1844. Aided by massive German immigration, the prelate developed the frontier diocese into one of the largest in the Midwest. Henni was elevated to the archbishopric in 1875.

A few of the Swiss in Wisconsin ventured beyond their own linguistic bounds to take the Gospel to the Indians in the state. Jakob Stucki (1857–1930), a Reformed minister, is the best known of these apostles. A native of the canton of Bern, he emigrated in 1873 and received basic theological training at a seminary in Plymouth, Wisconsin. In 1884 the Reformed Church commissioned Stucki to teach at a school for the Winnebago near Black River Falls to which he devoted nearly half a century of his life. The young missionary soon discovered that he had taken up a heavy cross. "The language of the Winnebagoes is still quite undeveloped and therefore extremely difficult to learn," he lamented in the 1890s. Stucki consoled himself with the knowledge that "even the Jesuits are said to have given up learning it." He eventually mastered Winnebago, though, and translated the Bible into that tongue. Evangelizing the tribe demanded no less patience than did language study; not until 1897 could Stucki baptize his first four converts. The school with which he was so closely affiliated was moved to Neillsville in 1921.

PATRIOTISM TESTED

It is impossible to discern how large a proportion of the Swiss in Wisconsin supported the American entry into World War I or to what extent German immigrant opposition to intervention influenced them. In Green County, at any rate, patriotism appears to have been quite strong despite initial misgivings. C. H. Hefty, the village president of New Glarus, reminded the community on April 12, 1917, six days after Congress had answered President Wilson's plea to make the world "safe for democracy" by declaring war on the Central Powers, that "it is the duty of every American citizen to stand by his government." Those of New Glarus had apparently not been of one mind on the issue. "Whatever our individual ideas or feelings may be with regard to the war, the time for arguments is now past," admonished Hefty, "and as loyal American citizens we should refrain from disputing the matter in private and publicly."

The community heeded his entreaty and bowed to the will of the county draft board. Seventy-three men of New Glarus were inducted into the armed forces. Seventy-one of them returned alive.

VITAL AND RESPECTED CITIZENS

The Swiss played a supporting role in Wisconsin's historical pageant, as did most other immigrants and their descendants. Few trod with Emanuel Philipp into the limelight. Their place was in the background, where they served the other members of the cast by milking cows, repairing machinery, keeping shops, and performing a wide variety of other services in their predominantly rural areas. Yet theirs is a revealing story for students of immigration. As late as 1947, *National Geographic* magazine featured New Glarus and environs as a unique region of cultural retention. Its saga of a cohesive settlement in a relatively isolated area upholding many Old World folkways while vigorously participating in the life of the New richly deserves the attention that historians, anthropologists, and others have given it.

The story of the Swiss who found homes in areas where they were a small minority yields more subtle but equally valuable lessons. That their native languages were spoken in different dialects by far more numerous neighbors from other lands presumably hastened their assimilation, but it also militated against preserving their national or cantonal identity. These Swiss thus found themselves in situations roughly parallel to those of many Belgian, Austrian, and Scottish newcomers. Regardless of the pace at which they consciously or unconsciously shed their identity, however, the Swiss were rapidly integrated as vital and respected residents of rural Wisconsin.

WHi Image ID 25785

The rugged Mississippi River bluffs overlooking Fountain City, and on northward through Buffalo County, drew many Swiss immigrants who were used to terrain such as that surrounding the village of Zermatt in southern Valais near the Matterhorn.

WHi Image ID 43988

Zermatt, Switzerland, about 1890.

WHi Image ID 42739

Newly arrived Swiss immigrants, photographed by John Luchsinger in New Glarus about 1905.

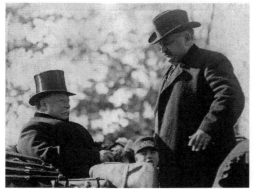

Left: Governor Emanuel L. Philipp with President Taft in Milwaukee, 1908 or 1910.

Below: Frontispiece from the Swiss passport issued November 22, 1848, to Benedict Goldenberger in the Canton of Aargau. Goldenberger left Switzerland in 1851, stopping first in Massachusetts before moving to Madison in 1857.

Right: Four women in Swiss costume display flags at New Glarus's Wilhelm Tell Festival (undated).

WHi Image ID 42633

WHi Image ID 42749

The Swiss Reformed Church in New Glarus (undated).

Poster for New Glarus's 1931 "Swiss Day Celebration."

WHi Image ID 44075

New Glarus yodelers (undated).

WHi Image ID 44005

WHi Image ID 43998

Green County women and children in Swiss costume (undated).

WHi Image ID 43999

The Alma Shooting Society, a Swiss "schutenfest" club affiliated with the Central Shooting Society of Wisconsin, about 1910.

Swiss musicians Otto and Iva Rindlisbacher with their instruments, 1920.

WHi Image ID 45270

Left: Two women display fascinating Swiss costumes at New Glarus's Wilhelm Tell Festival, 1941.

Below: The alpenhorn, or alphorn, was used by herders in the Alps to call livestock to pasture. These Monroe women in Swiss costume demonstrate a large alphorn, 1955.

WHi Image ID 43995

THE PLANTING OF THE SWISS COLONY
AT NEW GLARUS, WIS.

BY JOHN LUCHSINGER

Collections of the State Historical Society of Wisconsin, 12:340–365

This entry in the Collections of the State Historical Society of Wisconsin *comes from John Luchsinger, who was born in the canton of Glarus, Switzerland, in 1839 and moved to America at age six. He settled, along with many of his fellow Swiss, at New Glarus in 1856. This passage represents a second chronicle of the colony's beginnings. The first, written in 1879 and appearing in volume 8 of the* Wisconsin Historical Collections, *was the earliest monograph about the young colony of Swiss immigrants. The passages included here provide insight into the motives for making such a monumental move without much guarantee for a better life. The complete texts of both memoirs are available for free online, in the digital edition of the* Wisconsin Historical Collections *(www.wisconsinhistory.org).*

CAUSES OF EMIGRATION

The causes which led to the establishment of this colony of New Glarus were mainly overpopulation in an unfertile country, and the poverty resulting from scarcity of employment and food. Prior to the year 1844, there was an era of uncommon prosperity throughout Europe. A long peace following the destructive wars of Napoleon had repeopled the nations, had rebuilt the cities, and restored confidence in the business world. Trade and manufactures had greatly increased, the latter particularly in Switzerland, where the numberless swift mountain streams afford unlimited and cheap propelling power for machinery, and where the supply of labor is cheap and abundant. The large numbers of young Swiss who formerly were compelled to seek work in foreign lands found employment in these home industries. No longer was Switzerland the recruiting ground for the armies of Europe. The country needed the blood and brains and muscle, and enlistments were forbidden by Swiss law. This was a golden era; everyone prospered, and the people were content to remain in the land of their birth. But about 1844 a general stagnation in business occurred, overproduction of manufactures glutted the markets, and the trade in and demand for Swiss goods declined; large numbers of workmen were thrown out of employment. In addition to this, a partial failure of the Swiss crops caused the necessities of life to rise in price, distress became general and great among the working classes, and it became a serious question how to employ and feed the ever-increasing population.

In some parts of Switzerland, the land fit for cultivation is very limited in extent, and is owned by the different municipalities. It is divided into greater or smaller parcels according to the number of adult male citizens, and these parcels are annually allotted for the purpose of cultivation, free of charge. As the population increases the parcels become smaller, so that at this time in Glarus they ranged from one hundred and sixty to six hundred and forty square yards for the head of each family, according as the parish to which he belonged was rich or poor. In many instances the parishes also own the forests, and the summer pastures on the Alps, which are leased from time to time to dairymen. The income from these sources is applied to defray in part the public expenses, including the support of schools and churches; in consequence, taxation is light. Every citizen in Glarus is entitled to the use of one of these portions of tillable land, which he may cultivate by himself or by proxy. When a citizen emigrates, the value of his allotment , together with the value of his interest of in the rest of the common property, is estimated, and paid to him in money. Practically, this is selling out his vested rights in the property of the community, and amounts really to a premium on emigration. These small parcels are mainly planted with potatoes, beans, or other annual crops. The authorities are so careful of the food supply, that on these allotments no one is allowed to dig even his own potatoes until they are fully ripe. As the harvest approaches, watchmen are employed day and night to guard the crop, and a heavy fine is imposed upon the luckless individual who may be detected in gratifying his relish for new potatoes before the law has pronounced them ripe. The production of grain is quite impossible, — there is not enough land fit for such crops, and the use of horses, plows, and machinery is almost unknown. The people depend for bread-stuffs on Russia, Italy, and Hungary. Hence bread is seldom cheap. In ordinary and even prosperous times, the supply in most families is limited. The poor are seldom able to eat as much as they desire. In times of depression, the food of the working classes is mainly potatoes, with salt or green cheese (called *schabzieger*) for seasoning.

Coffee is made mainly from chicory and is used without sugar, and often without milk. Close economy in everything, from the smallest to the greatest article of food, clothing, or other necessity, is rigidly required by the conditions of the surroundings, in order to be able to exist. A wasteful person is regarded as almost criminal.

Even such economy as this could not prevent the distress and impoverishment from becoming alarming, when in 1844 the great sources of income dried up — the factories having either ceased work or shortened time and wages. The authorities and leading citizens of Glarus cast about for ways and means by which the consequent distress could be relieved. Public meetings were held to discuss the subject of emigration as a remedy. The matter was discussed pro and con in every cottage and household. The timid and conservative freely quoted the old saying, *"Bleibet im land und Ernahre dich redlich"* (Remain in the land and support yourself honestly). But the courageous and progressive invented another saying to match it, *"Bleibet im land und fresset einander"* (Remain in the land and devour each other). The prospect was, that the latter saying was in a fair way to be exemplified. Human labor was daily becoming plentier and cheaper, and food scarcer and dearer.

SELECTION OF A SITE

The agitation finally culminated in the idea that an organized emigration, under the care and control of the government, would be the best, surest, and most reliable method of affording the necessary relief. At a public meeting called at Schwanden, a committee was appointed to confer with and ask the aid and co-operation of the government of the canton. The council of the canton approved of the project so far as to appropriate fifteen hundred florins (about six hundred dollars), for the purpose of sending to America — as children of Israel did to the land of Canaan — two men who were to view the country, and if they found it suitable, to locate a tract favorable for a colony. An Emigration Society was at the same time formed, composed of intelligent and prominent men, who took charge of this fund, which was increased by subscription form the parishes and individuals to two thousand dollars. This society appointed as pioneers to look up a location, Judge Nicholas Duerst, then forty-eight years old, and Fridolin Streiff, a blacksmith, twenty-nine years old, both of them men of courage and endurance, and of more than average intelligence. Duerst agreed to assist in selecting and purchasing the lands for the colony, and to advise and remain with the colonists until they were fairly planted in their new home. Streiff was to remain three years with the colony, and to direct and control its work, and also to extend his assistance and counsel to all requiring it. He was also expend properly, for the benefit of the colony, whatever funds were placed in his hands for that purpose. Before the three years had expired, Streiff, with wise foresight, saw that the colony would succeed, and sent for his wife and children to join him. Previous to the appointment of Streiff, the society had appointed M. Mari, a teacher, as Judge Duerst's companion, for the reason that he had some knowledge of the English tongue, but his timidity and indecision were such that he withdrew on the very eve of departure, and Streiff was thereupon selected. To supply the defect of their ignorance of the English language, the pioneers were authorized to employ a competent interpreter on their arrival in America. All these preparations, because of their strangeness and novelty, consumed so much time that it was not until March 8, 1845, that the two leaders were able to start on their journey in search of a new home.

They carried with them the written instructions of the society, as follows: The two pioneers are to depart immediately, so as to be in time to embark on the packet ship which leaves Havre, France, on the sixteenth of March.[1] Drafts to the amount of six thousand, three hundred and sixty florins (about two thousand, six hundred dollars), being sixty florins for each of the one hundred and six prospective emigrants enrolled, for the purchase of the necessary land, will be placed in their hands. These funds they are, however, not draw upon until the purchase of the lands has been completed. On their arrival in New York they are to proceed without delay to William H. Blumer, a fellow Swiss, living in Allentown, Pennsylvania and request him to support them with his counsel and experience in exploration, and to assist them in making the purchase of land. In retrospect to this purchase, they are to consider particularly the instruction: that the locality chosen shall be similar to that of Glarus in climate, soil, and general characteristics. That the soil shall be suitable for raising stock, vegetables, fruit and grains. They are not bound strictly to purchase government land. If they deem it best to purchase a portion partly cultivated, they may do so; but they shall strictly keep in mind that

[1] There were no railroads in Switzerland at that time, and only for a short distance in France; hence eight days were allowed for the journey from Glarus through France to Havre.

each colonist shall have for his sixty florins, twenty acres of land, or nearly that area. They shall endeavor to purchase land in one body, and shall duly consider communication with other inhabited portions of the country, such as by roads, streams, railroads, etc. After completing the purchase, the tract is to be so divided that each colonist shall receive a proper proportion of timber, pasture, and tillable land. The respective portions shall be assigned to the colonists on their arrival, and the pioneers shall cause the proper surveys to be made, and shall immediately prepare for the reception of the first lot of colonists, who are to wait at St. Louis for further directions. They shall provide shelter, food, and clothing for the immediate needs of the colonists, and shall charge the same to their account. There shall be provision made immediately for the cultivation of grain for the use of the people, and the necessary number of cattle shall be provided. It might be of advantage, these careful instructions say, to at first cultivate a small portion of land in common, and then to assign each colonist a portion of the produce. This plan might be the most speedy to provide necessary food for all. The purchase of land shall be in the name of the Emigration Society of the Canton of Glarus. Duerst shall prepare a vital record, numbered according to number of colonists, and note all deaths or increase, giving dates. The pioneers shall endeavor to use their influence with the colonists, to the end that a church and schools may be established as soon as practicable; that the poor, sick, widows, and orphans may be relieved; and that the rules of the Emigration Society be observed and executed. The society shall be the owner of the lands until the sum advanced shall be repaid by the colonists. Duerst shall receive for his services one dollar per day, and his necessary traveling expenses. Streiff shall receive free passage to the settlement, and free entertainment until the departure of Duerst. For his other services, he shall be paid such a compensation as Duerst shall recommend to be proper. Duerst shall keep a correct daily journal of the traveling and other expenses.

Instructed, fortified, and also hindered in a measure, by these rules, the two pioneers embarked at Havre on the sixteenth of March, 1845, and after a tedious and stormy passage in a sailing packet arrived in New York on the sixth of May. On the tenth of May, they were joined at Easton, Pennsylvania, by Joshua Frey, whom Blumer had selected as their guide on account of his intelligence, and knowledge of the usages and language of the country. Frey kept a journal, in which he made daily en-

tries of the doings of the trio, and from which it appears that without farther delay they proceeded in the mail coach to Somerville, New York,
and from thence by railroad to New York city, and on the same day went
by steamer "Empire" to Albany, thence again by rail to Buffalo, at which
place they arrived May 14.

The diary states as follows: "Took passage on steamer Bunker Hill
for Detroit same evening, arrived at Detroit May 16. Next day proceeded
across the state of Michigan by stage and rail to St. Joseph. Thence by
steamer to Chicago, arriving there on the morn of the nineteenth. We
went to the United States land office in that town and examined the
maps and plats, and found that nearly all timber land in that land district
was either pre-empted or sold, but a great amount of prairie land was yet
open for entry. Next day took stage for Dixon, on Rock River. On the
way we crossed immense prairies, reaching an unbroken level so far as
the eye could see. The mail road passes through Aurora, the neighbor-
hood of which is quite well settled. Arrived at Dixon, May 21, having
rode all night. We went to the United States land office and found an immense quantity of prairie land yet subject to entry, but the woodland was
mostly taken. The same afternoon we traveled northward along Rock
river to Oregon city. May 23, we again returned to Dixon. The land on
both sides of Rock river is very fine and productive. May 24, we went by
stage to Princeton, a little village surrounded by rich lands. 25th, being
Sunday, we rested. 26th, examined a tract of timber known as Devil's
Grove, but found that it was already entered; could have bought 240 acres
for $1000. 27th, went to Peru on the Illinois river. 28th, as the water was
too low in the river for boats to land, we hired a team to take us to Hen-
nepin. 30th, went on steamer to St. Louis, where we arrived June 1. As
the expected emigrants had not yet come, we authorized Mr. Wild
of that city to take charge of them when they arrived, to send us word of
their arrival, and to provide temporary quarters for them."

The journal then relates in detail the travels of the three men by
stage, horseback, and on foot through Missouri, touching St. Charles,
Warrenton, Danville, Mexico, Florida, Palmyra, and Marion. From
Marion they took the steamer "Di Vernon" to Keokuk, in Iowa Territory,
then across the country to Winchester, Fairfield, and Mt. Pleasant, spend-
ing some time at the United States land office at Fairfield; thence east-
ward to Bloomington, on the Mississippi; thence to Galena, "which is a
town of considerable importance, the head of navigation, and the cen-

tre of the lead-mining region. Although we had traveled now through a
number of states, we had not yet decided to buy anywhere, for the reason either that wood or water was wanting, the location unhealthy, or not
a sufficient tract of suitable land in one body; so we traveled farther into
Wisconsin Territory, touching Platteville and Belmont, and arriving at
Mineral Point June 16. At the land office, we really found a prospect to
make suitable selections. Having at this place received a letter from Mr.
Blumer, stating that the emigrants might be expected at Milwaukee, we
at once proceeded to that place, but were disappointed. At the Milwaukee land office we found, after examination, that the land in that district
was not favorable for our emigrants. On the 24th of June, we therefore
left Milwaukee via Troy, to Exeter, in Green county. Here, at last, we
found in town 4, range 7, a large extent of land suitable for our purposes,
containing the prescribed qualities, as: healthy climate, copious springs,
fertile soil, timber, and prospect of convenient market for produce. After
several more fruitless trips in different directions southward to Como,
Illinois, and northwest to the Wisconsin river, we returned to Mineral
Point, where we met Theodore Rodolf, who received us kindly and gave
us his advice and help, and accompanied us on several trips in this
district. On our return to Mineral Point, on July 17, we finally concluded
to purchase near Exeter, Green county, twelve hundred acres of the land
we had seen on June 27, and in addition eighty acres of good timber. We
further bought necessary provisions and tools, with which we at once proceeded to the colony land, and Duerst and Streiff began to build huts.
On the twenty-fourth of July the surveyor arrived, and with the kind help
of Frederick Rodolf,[2] a brother of Theodore, we finished the survey and
also the building of two temporary huts on the 30th." At this point, Frey's
journal closes with the remark that on the sixth of August he bade
farewell to Messrs. Duerst and Streiff, and departed for his home in
Pennsylvania.

Judge Duerst wrote on August 19th, 1845, to the Emigration Society,
Switzerland: "We have selected and bought what we believe to be a
favorable point for settlement. The land lies eight miles from Exeter, and
thirty-five miles from Mineral Point, where great markets are held. It con-
tains mostly fertile soil, good water in springs and streams, and sufficient
forests. One of the streams running through our land has sufficient power

2 Still living at South Wayne, Wisconsin.

for one or two mills, and we indulge in the pleasing hope that our fellow-citizens who may emigrate, will, if they are industrious and steady, find themselves in time well rewarded for their labor. The colonists, one hundred and eight souls, have arrived after a long journey, in which they experienced many hardships and disappointments, and are so destitute of everything that we were at once obliged to draw upon our credit in New York, so as to be able to supply their needs until the next harvest. We have provided temporary shelters for them, and have allotted the parcels of land to each colonist. Have also drawn rules and by-laws for the government of the colony, and for best managing its possessions, and have elected four trustees — Fridolin Streiff, Balthasar Schindler, Fridolin Babler, and David Schindler, the last-named to act as secretary."

Some of the regulations laid down for the management of the colony are worthy to be recorded as curiosities: "Section I. — Every one is obliged to take the land which he draws by lot, and whether it be better or sores to accept the same without protest. Section II. — The main street from east to west shall be thirty feet wide, but the other streets shall be only fourteen feet wide.[3] Further, all creeks, streams, and springs shall be the common property of all lot owners. The colonists shall be obliged to assist each other in building houses and barns. As soon as the patents for the lands shall have been signed by the president of the United States, and not before, each owner shall have the right to dig and prospect for mineral. Should such be found, then the lot on which it is found shall revert to the society, and the owner shall receive therefor[e] an appropriate compensation."

Of course these and other regulations from the same source were operative only for a short time, and until the people had become acquainted with the laws and customs of this country which govern such matters. Taking everything into consideration, in the light of better judgment and later experience, a better location might have been selected, — richer, deeper, and more level soil, shorter distance to markets, and other advantages, could have been had a that time with little cost as the site chosen; but viewing the result, it is doubtful if under more favorable conditions a better or even as good showing would have been made. The mountaineer from old Glarus seems to have more readily taken root and

[3] This was bringing the narrow, contracted ideas of land in Switzerland, to the broad land of America, with a vengeance.

thriven on the rocky hillsides and pleasant valleys of New Glarus, than he would have done in what we now consider more favorable localities. The energy developed in subduing the rocky soil, and felling the gnarled timber, seemed to give its possessors an impetus that carried them to competence and prosperity with a force that hardly would have been developed under easier beginnings. Had the pioneers not literally followed the society's orders to purchase twelve hundred acres in one body, it would have been better, as much rough and worthless land was included, which could have been avoided and valuable land taken instead. But they thought themselves bound to follow their instructions strictly and conscientiously, and they deserve a full measure of approval for their work.

THE MIGRATION

And now to relate the story of the migration of the colonists to the place so selected for them. The society's committee was at first inclined to postpone the emigration until the spring of 1846, so as to give sufficient time for the pioneers to view the land, and, if a location was made, to make ample preparations for the reception of the people on their arrival. But the spirit of emigration had thoroughly permeated the whole community, and was at fever heat. The pressure was threatening to overthrow all the nicely considered plans for an organized emigration. To avoid the consequences of a threatened irregular exodus, and in order to retain control of the movement, the committee was compelled to act promptly. The sixteenth of April, 1845, was therefore fixed upon for the departure. On account of the number of emigrants and the amount of their baggage, the water route down the Rhine to Rotterdam was determined upon, and preparations made accordingly. The emigrants were notified to assemble, and hold themselves in readiness to embark at the time stated; and the respective amounts necessary to defray the passage and expenses were to be paid into a common fund, either by the colonists themselves or, when unable, by the parishes to which they belonged. The whole scheme resembled stock company, and each emigrant represented a share and was assessed in proportion for all expenses.[4]

In the night of April 15–16, the arrangements were finally completed,

---

[4] The reader cannot fail to note strong points of unconscious resemblance between this organization and that of the Pilgrim Fathers, two and a quarter centuries before. — Ed.

and on the morning of the sixteenth the committee proceeded the place of departure, — the so-called "Biäsche," a landing place on the Linth canal, which runs alongside the Linth river, a tributary of the Rhine in Glarus. On the banks of this canal, on this gloomy April morning, one hundred and ninety-three persons of all ages and conditions were collected in the pelting rain. Only one hundred and forty had been expected and provided for, but the desire to emigrate under the protection of an organization had become so great that almost at the last moment fifty-three more had, unannounced, joined, the party and determined to share its fortunes. Such were the colonists who were in readiness to venture into that strange, far-off land, called America, of which they had read and spoken, heard and dreamed so much, It was said to be the home and refuge of the poor, where those who came with stout hands and willing hearts were sure eventually to reap a rich reward, and where, better than all, their children would have bread enough to eat. Yet among all those who were ready and anxious to leave, few could look back upon the frowning, yet beloved mountains, on whose rugged sides they had left their poor homes, and humble but kind friends and kindred, without feeling that their courage was tried to the utmost. But the thought gave them firmness, that in the beautiful land they were leaving, increasing and hopeless poverty was ever present, and want and oppression were the lot of the poor, with no ray of hope for the better.

With tearful eyes and hearts full of grief, they took their last leave of friends and fatherland; and with few earthly goods, but rich in firm resolves and hopes, they embarked in an open barge. Before starting, Landamman C. Jenny,[5] representing the government of the canton of Glarus, addressed the colonists in words full of feeling. He urged upon them the necessity of industry, harmony, and unity; and commending them to the care of kind Providence, bade them God-speed and farewell. And so, amid the tears and kind wishes of an immense concourse of friends and relatives, the boat-load of emigrants started on their way and slowly began a wearisome journey towards an unknown land. At the start, the colonists chose two of their number, George Legler and Jacob Grob, to act as leaders and spokesmen during the migration, to exercise general care and supervision over everything connected with the journey, to preserve order, and to hear and redress all complaints. The colonists

[5] Died at Glarus, May 25, 1892.

on their part promised to obey the directions and abide by the decisions of these leaders.

Before reaching Zurich, the weather had become inclement and mow fell, the closely-packed open vessel soon becoming uncomfortable and unfit for the passage of so many. So inadequate was the space, in consequence of the unexpected addition to the number of the company, that there was no room to lie down; and when night came, those who could slept as well as possible in a sitting posture. At Zurich, it became evident that this crowded condition must be relieved, or great distress would prevail, especially among the women and children. The Swiss bundesrath was at that time in session at Zurich, and the Glarus representative, Cosmos Blumer, kindly provided teams and covered wagons, in which the women and children found more comfortable passage, and in which they followed the vessel on shore until they all reached Basle, about fifty miles from Glarus. Mathias Duerst, one of the number, a man of more than ordinary intelligence and a close observer, kept a diary of the events on the journey, from which the author will freely quote.[6]

Says Duerst: "We arrived at Basle on the 18th. The cold rain was falling in streams, and the utter wretchedness and discomfort were enough to chill the ardor of the strongest among us wet, shivering men. The wagons containing our wives and children arrived about the same time; and although they had been packed in like a lot, of goods, we were glad that they had not been exposed to the cold and wet as we had been."

On the nineteenth, the emigrants again embarked, this time on a steamboat on the Rhine. The boat ran only in the daytime, and stopped every night, usually at some town or village, where the men would get out and purchase provisions for the next day, — for only the passage had been contracted for; every one had to provide food as best he could, whenever opportunity offered. There were no berths or beds on the boat, and sleep was had either on the bare planks of the vessel's deck or in such lodging-houses at the stopping places as could harbor the crowd at cheap rates. In this comfortless, wearisome manner, they proceeded down the Rhine northward. Loud and deep were the murmurs of discontent and exasperation at the want of consideration and business tact of those who had contracted the expedition of the emigrants in this slow, miserable

[6] It has been kindly loaned to the author by Miss Salome Duerst, a sister of Mathias, and herself one of the few surviving pioneer colonists.

manner; and it sometimes required the utmost tact and persuasion on the part of the leaders, to preserve the peace and prevent open mutiny and disorder. What at first appeared the cheapest route proved, in consequence of the delays and increased cost of subsistence, to be by far the dearest.

At last, on the thirtieth of April, they arrived at Rotterdam, where they were loaded on two coasting vessels, wherein they were to be carried to New Dieppe, the seaport, In the night a severe storm arose, which lasted until the morning. It was a terrible experience, for none of the colonists were accustomed to the sea. May 2, they arrived at New Dieppe, and at once went on board of the ocean vessel, which was a fine three-master with eighty-eight berths. On the third they bought straw for their berths, and could now for the fist time sleep with some comfort; but as no cooking arrangements had yet been placed in the ship, they were obliged to kindle fires on the land, and cook outdoors, in gypsy fashion. Owing to the ship's incomplete accomodations for carrying passengers, the company was delayed until the thirteenth, on which day the ship weighed anchor, and the departing Swiss bade farewell to Europe — nearly all of them forever. A tug pulled the vessel out about six miles, when her sails were set, and day by day she plowed her way westward, sometimes tossed by storms and again almost becalmed.

At that period, on sailing vessels, each passenger or family cooked his or their own food, and among a large number of passengers the difficulty of getting a chance to cook in the one small kitchen was often extreme. The strong and healthy came first, the weakly were crowded out; during storms no fires were permitted, and the passengers were sometimes from four to five days without warm food or drink. The sick and the children suffered terribly at such times. The miserable ship biscuit was as fit for food as so much leather. Those who had dried meats and fruits, or cheese, fared quite well, but others suffered from hunger. Two and a half pounds of salt pork, a half pound of flour, two pounds of rice, and as much ship biscuit as could be used, were the weekly ration for each full passenger.

On the twenty-eighth, the company were saddened by two deaths, the wife of Rudolf Stauffacher, and a six-months-old child of Henry Stauffacher; they died within a few hours of each other, and in less than two hours after their death were wound in sheets, weighted with sand, and after a short burial service read by Jacob Grob, were sunk into the trackless ocean. The wretched quality of the food dealt out to the emigrants had by this time occasioned diarrhea and dysentery among many. All were so weakened that despondency and discontent prevailed, and many the complaints and quarrels which the leaders were called upon to hear and quell. But in time more contentment prevailed, for complaints did not mend matters.

On the twenty eighth and twenty-ninth of June, land was in sight. The warm American air seemed to be full of reviving qualities, the sick grew better, the despondent gained courage; and when on the thirtieth day of June, after a voyage of forty-nine days full of storms and hardships, the vessel landed at Baltimore, all were on their feet cleansed and dressed in their best, ready and impatient to greet their adopted land and to found new homes in the then far west. The orders were, that the emigrants should proceed to St. Louis, where directions would be found to guide them to the selected locality. After some discussion, it was voted, in view of the miserable treatment on shipboard, that the firm to whom they were directed by the shippers at Rotterdam to apply for further transportation, were unworthy of confidence, and a committee of three were selected to contract for the passage to St. Louis. This, in view of the fact that an immense amount of extra baggage was to be transported, was a difficult matter. The emigrants and their friends, in their ignorance of the extent and resources of this county, had taken along not only their clothing and bedding, but also their kitchen and table furniture, pots, pans, and kettles, and the mechanics had complete kits of tools. The belief was, that even should it be found that America could supply such articles, they would be much inferior to those brought from the old country. Thus there were many thousands of pounds of excess baggage to provide for. A contract was finally made with a Jew, to carry the company to St. Louis for twenty dollars each adult; children from four to twelve years were rated at half-fare; those younger than four years were to be carried free; while the excess baggage was to be charged for at the rate of a dollar per hundred weight. These negotiations took several days.

On the fourth of July, Mathias Duerst states in his diary: "We saw the most imposing ceremony that any of us ever saw in our lives. If was the funeral obsequies of the former president of the nation, Gen. Jackson. The space in my whole diary would be too small to describe the splendors and the solemnities we witnessed. Thousands on thousands of horsemen were in the procession, and the honors done to the memory of the great man who, like Cincinnatus, was several times called from the plow to the head of the nation, were impressive and grand. At this point, two of our families not having been provided with any means for further travel, made known their condition to the leaders, and it was determined to advance them fifteen dollars each out of the small relief fund of the colony, so as to provide them with food until the men could get employment, which they accepted with many thanks, and they remained at Baltimore."

Later, Duerst writes: "On the fifth of July, one mile out of the city, we got on the cars for the first time. Then we experienced the greatest pleasure in our lives. None of us had ever before rode on a, railroad. We passed with the speed of the wind through splendid fields and wooded valleys. The eye feasted on rapid changes, on rich grain fields, and fruitful orchards; and then we went by tasty, elegant dwellings. All this proclaimed American wealth and prosperity to us, and the troubles and hardships of the weeks just passed were forgotten in the hope that some day we might call a like-appearing country our home. The train took us to the Susquehanna river at Columbia, where we left the cars and loaded our baggage and persons on the canal boats which were to carry us to Pittsburgh. These were totally inadequate for our numbers. We were packed in like a herd of sheep. Thirty to thirty-five human beings were put in a space twelve by seven feet; many could not even sit, but had to stand up the whole night. In the morning, more boats were provided. They were drawn by one horse each, and we had plenty of time to step out and buy milk or other provisions, the speed was so slow, and the stoppages many. At Hollidaysburg, the canal terminated; our boats with all their contents were loaded on an iron track and drawn up the steep mountain side by a wire rope attached to a steam-engine on the top, and were conveyed down on the other side, sometimes with horses and engines, and sometimes of our own motion. At Johnstown, our boats again were let into the canal, and proceeded as before, It is astonishing what works these Americans have performed."

Duerst further says: "We passed through a delightful region, smiling with productiveness and plenty, log-houses alternating with fine mansions, and women in good clothes and bonnets on were milking cows; but this is about all the work they do, so far as I saw, for we perceived even in the log-houses that they sat in rocking chairs, clothed with bonnets and shawls, with arms crossed, sitting like noble ladies."

At Pittsburgh, on the evening of the tenth, they embarked on a steamboat, and steamed down the Ohio river, "'Excepting that the wife of one of our emigrants gave birth to a fine boy, on the first night, and that our steamer ran aground while racing with another, there was nothing worthy of mention." The captain of the vessel, through an interpreter, informed himself of the purpose of the emigrants, and bluntly told them they were fools to make such a journey for the sake of getting twenty acres of land with the privilege of paying for it — that twenty acres in this country was nothing; it was not worth while building a house on. In a few years, by working at their trades or occupations, they could save enough money to buy ten times that amount of land. When the emigrants would not be dissuaded from their set purpose, he indignantly turned his back, and said he would not waste more words on such fools. At Cincinnati, three of the company tired of the seemingly endless journey, and were persuaded by friends living at that place to remain; several had already dropped off at Pittsburgh, in the same way. The wonder is, under the circumstances, that more did not detach themselves, especially those who were mechanics, for wages in the cities were about two dollars a day for skilled labor, and food and clothing were then very cheap. Nothing seemed, however, to be able to turn the main body from their purpose. The summer heat by day, the torment of myriads of mosquitoes by night, the crowded quarters, and the inferior food, were not calculated to elevate their spirits; but notwithstanding all this, their courage did not give out. On the nineteenth there was another birth of a boy, the third since leaving home.

On the twenty-third, the company of Swiss emigrants arrived at St. Louis. Here they expected to meet their pioneers, Streiff and Duerst, or at least to find the promised instructions from them; but neither the pioneers nor letters from them, were at St. Louis. There was nothing but a letter from Mr. Blumer, of Allentown, in which he informed them that the pioneers were on the search for land, somewhere in Illinois; but the letter was a month old, and gave no definite information. On the other hand, rumors circulated that the two pioneers had while exploring lost their lives. In the midst of conflicting stories of all kinds, the party and their leaders were in extreme anxiety. Undecided which way to turn, they rented two houses, in which they crowded for temporary shelter, meeting daily for mutual counsel. Some of the party earned a few dollars at odd jobs of work. The suspense finally became unbearable, and on the twenty-fifth it was determined that two of their number, Paulus Grob and

Mathias Duerst, should proceed to search for the pioneers. They found a steamer ready to start for Peoria and other points on the Illinois river, and took deck passage, but were obliged on account of the intolerable plague of mosquitoes to change to cabin accommodations before going far. They arrived at Peoria on the night of the thirty-first, but found no tidings. Following a chance hint in Blumer's letter, they proceeded to Peru, Illinois, seventy-five miles across the country. The fare on the steamer was four dollars, which was more money than they had, and they went most of the way on foot.

They relate that immense tracts of prairie were still wild, unenclosed, and open for entry and sale, and they were charmed by the beauty and productiveness of the country. They were hospitably entertained by the settlers on the way, and Duerst relates in his diary: "Every one seems to live in plenty. The tables in the lowliest cabins are as well if not better supplied than those of the best hotels in Switzerland, and the surprise is that they can live in this way, and yet it is said the people only work about one-fourth of the year; the rest of the year they go hunting, or follow such other amusement as they please. The cattle are no trouble; when night comes, they come of themselves to the dwellings, and so many of the cows are milked as is necessary for the wants of the family, and no more. Sheep cost no more than their wool would bring. This seems like a country of marvelous plenty, and the people are extremely friendly."

They arrived at Peru on the third of August, and on inquiry at the post-office found that the pioneers had been there, had gone to Mineral Point, Wisconsin, and had requested the post-master to forward all mail for them to that locality. This was depressing news. The little money the men had was gone, and it would cost twelve dollars to carry them to Galena, Out of this dilemma they were lifted by a fellow Swiss, John Freuler, who was working at Peru; he generously loaned them the necessary sum until such time as they could repay him. They wrote to St. Louis what the situation was, and hired a team and driver. Duerst thus describes the outfit: "The wagon was a miserable affair without springs, and covered with a torn, dirty rag, but the horses were splendid, fit for princes; it is just the reverse of what it is in the old home. There the carriages are fine and grand, but the horses are miserable things. We fairly flew across the wide prairies, which seemed as wide as the ocean — nothing but sky and grass, no shrub, tree, or human being to be seen.'"

On the sixth, they reached Galena, and proceeded northward

through the lead-mine region into Wisconsin, traveling mostly on foot, and arriving at Mineral Point next day at 9 o'clock in the evening. In answer to anxious inquiries, they learned that the pioneers were yet thirty-five miles farther on, that they had bought land, and were awaiting the colonists, of whom they had no information, and knew not in what direction to look for them, They determined to go forward, and a helpful German found a team and driver for them, promising to see that it was paid for until they could repay him. They rode twenty-five miles, when darkness overtook them and they were obliged, despite their impatience, to stop overnight with a settler. They found, too, they had missed the direct road. Next day they proceeded, and about 2 o'clock in the afternoon stopped at another house, here finding that those they sought were still four miles off. The teamster, desiring to return to Mineral Point, refused to go farther, and the men were obliged to travel on foot in the direction indicated. In due time they saw through an opening in the timber, first some huts, and then men at work. The latter approached, and in these they found the long-sought pioneers and friends, As all clasped hands, with tears of joy springing to their eyes, their feelings may better be imagined than described. The joy of that first meeting was something to be remembered by all, so long as life lasted.

The new comers were first refreshed with food and drink, and then shown over the new possession. To their eyes it seemed, a splendid sight. Hills and valleys, woods, prairies, and streams, seemed in just the right proportion, all being glorified in the brilliant light of that August day. A halo was cast over all imperfections; in the eyes of the weary wanderers, all things in this land of promise were perfect. It was at once decided that some me should go to St. Louis and guide the other colonists hither. The new comers were anxious to remain and assist in the work of building shelters. Judge Duerst was therefore requested to go for the colonists, and left at once. He arrived at Galena on the evening of the next day, intending there to take river passage to St. Louis. Early next morning he went to the steamboat landing. While there, some one casually remarked that a large party of immigrants had arrived the evening before from St. Louis on the very steamer on which he was about to take down passage. Curiosity caused him to make further inquiries, when to his astonishment he found that those whom he was going to escort from St. Louis had arrived. The delight of this meeting can well be imagined.

All were eager to leave immediately for their new home. Duerst directed that the able-bodied men should start in advance, and assist in preparing for the reception and shelter of the main body, while he would make some necessary arrangements and purchases, and follow as soon as possible. On the afternoon of the same day, eighteen men started on foot for the settlement, a distance of sixty-two miles. Such was their eagerness, that they traveled all night and the next day, without stopping, except to partake of food. On the evening of the second day, they arrived at Wiota, in LaFayette county. There they obtained lodging for the night in a stable. There was no road in the direction of the settlement, so procuring a guide, and buying some flour, and loading it on their backs, together with their tools and cooking utensils, they walked the rest of the way, arriving in the evening tired and footsore. They relate that every person whom they met or saw fled at their approach, and no wonder; for bearded, rough, and ragged as they were, loaded with all manner of baggage and tools, at a distance they more resembled a band of robbers than a party of honest immigrants.

Without delay the new comers began the building of a large hut, in addition to those already provided. A large excavation was made in the hillside, within the enclosure of what is now known as the old graveyard, close to the site of the present district school-house. Posts were set in the ground, and a roof made of boughs and wild hay; the sides were afterwards enclosed with boards hauled from Galena; the floor was at first the bare earth, this being afterwards covered with split poplar logs, the riven side uppermost; there were no windows or chimney. Some of the men were carpenters, all were workers, and the materials were close at hand, so that when in three days afterward all the colonists arrived they were passably sheltered, at least from wind and sun. Teams had been hired at Galena to convey the women, children, and provisions, but not in sufficient numbers, so that all except the smallest and weakest had to take turns in riding and walking. On the always-to-be-remembered fifteenth day of August, 1845, all of the colonists, except those who strayed on the way, were assembled in the promised land of New Glarus.

The entire journey of over five thousand miles had been made by water, except the distance from Baltimore to Columbia, and from Galena to New Glarus. Taking into account the time consumed, and the vexatious delays and hardships undergone, the journey seems to have a parallel only in the exodus of the Jews from Egypt to their promised land. Only a hundred and eight remained out of the original hundred and

ninety-three, the rest having from various causes deserted the party.
Many of these deserters, however, in after years rejoined the colony and
remained to share its labors and successes.

Sharing the then popular belief that America was mostly an uncul-
tivated wilderness, many of the colonists had, as I have before stated,
brought with them from Switzerland their tools, pats, pans, and kettles
of the old style, — heavy and unwieldy, but having the sterling quality of
durability. Despite the cost and trouble of transportation, it proved fortunate that they were brought; for in the utter absence of money at the
first, no one could have bought anything, and these implements did duty
for the whole settlement, being used in turn until each family had the
means to buy their own. When the colonists arrived at their location,
there was but little food on hand, except what they brought with them
from Galena. The streams abounded in fish, but hooks and lines were
few, so that one party was detailed to catch grasshoppers for bait, and another to catch fish. A large number were soon caught, but in the making
up of the supplies salt had been forgotten. Hunger and want, however,
are excellent cooks. The large hut answered the purpose of a shelter very
well in the day time and in fair weather; but at night and on rainy days
the inmates were crowded like sheep in a pen, to avoid the drip. New log
houses, sixteen in number, rude and simple, roofed with wild hay, and
capable of accommodating two families each, were put up as fast as possible. When Christmas arrived, the colony was fairly housed, and in a
measure prepared for winter.

TAKING ROOT

The beginning was now made. The land was bought and surveyed, but
the immediate prospect was dismal enough. Far away from communication with their old home, with neighbors who were strangers and looked
upon them with distrust; ignorant of the language, customs, manners,
and laws of the new country; knowing nothing of the prevalent mode of
cultivating the soil, and in want of proper clothing and the necessities of
life, it certainly was a dark outlook to these colonists. If it had not been
that the sum of a thousand dollars, provided in Switzerland for their assistance, arrived just at this time, it would indeed have gone hard with
them. This money, under the direction of the leaders, was wisely ex-
pended: a portion for food and clothing, and the remainder for stock of
various kinds.

Streiff wrote at this time to the Emigration Society: "I buy the provisions in large quantities and distribute them at cost, charging the amount to those who have no means, and receiving payment from those who are more fortunate. I supply all, even those who have means to buy, as they could not buy as cheaply themselves. Flour per cwt. costs two dollars, beef two and a half cents a lb. by the quarter, tallow four cents, lard four cents, and potatoes twenty-two cents per bushel. Should the people do well, I shall call upon them to repay these advances."

The first winter passed quietly. Beyond planning for the work of the coming season, and providing the necessary fuel, little could be done. In the spring, the colonists drew lots for their twenty-acre portions, which were mostly meadow or prairie land. The timber-lot of eighty acres, some two miles away, was held in common; for more than a year, each colonist used from it what he needed, and then it was divided into two-and-a-half-acre lots, one to go with each twenty-acre tract. If was agreed that the cost of the land at the time of purchase, together with advances made for any other purpose, should be repaid by the colonists without interest, within ten years. Should any person abandon or refuse to accept his tract, the next Swiss emigrant settler might take it. Only a few of these tracts were abandoned, and all were paid for before the ten years had expired.

It is proper to record a secession on a small scale. Small as the canton of Glarus is, ranges of lofty mountains divide it into two natural divisions, the Great and Little valleys. Each of these valleys, and in fact almost every village, has some peculiarity of language and customs, and the inhabitants of each section cherish a strong clannish feeling and affection for their own people. This clannish spirit, born in the valleys of the fatherland, showed itself from the start, in spite of their common interest in the present venture. Each group of colonists preferred to associate with their own valley people. This feeling was particularly strong among the Little-valley folk, perhaps because of the secluded location of their old home. About one-fourth of the settlers were from the Little-valley. Some matters of disagreement, trifling in themselves, caused a division, and this led to the secession of about twenty-five of these persons. A few weeks after their arrival, they erected a separate shelter for themselves on the east bank of the stream, about eighty rods from the main habitation, and close to the present bridge. But in the spring they rejoined the main body. Several of these same families, after a year or two, abandoned the colony altogether, and removed to larger tracts of land in the towns of Mt. Pleasant and Sylvester, some twelve miles distant, where there is now a prosperous and large settlement, mainly of Little-valley people. The younger portion of the community have, however, out-grown the old clannish distrust, and the two groups have become, through intermarriage and other social ties, united and harmonious.

After the allotment of the land had been made, each colonist began to clear and plow his tract, in which labor the women rendered assistance, as most of them were accustomed from childhood to outdoor work. At first the breaking was slow and laborious, being done with spades and shovels, for no teams or plows were obtained until later in the season. Potatoes, beans, and other vegetables were thus planted; and later, some sod corn. During the first spring (1846), drovers from Ohio brought droves of cows to Exeter. The colonists hearing of it set out to purchase, and being excellent judges of cattle soon selected the best animals of the herd, in sufficient numbers to give each family one. These cost twelve dollars per head, and were paid for out of the reserve fund before mentioned. Additional cabins were now built on a separate plat, so as to form a village, and each family soon had a home of its own. With a hut and a cow for each household, and vegetables growing, the frugal people began to feel contented and prosperous. Like a young tree the colony had at last taken root, and was growing.

Progress towards, prosperity and independence was naturally slow, because of want of adequate means to buy tools and stock, and ignorance in the manner of tilling the soil and taking care of crops after the methods of this country. Generally, in their native home, no horses or plows can be used in agriculture, — spading, sowing, mowing, etc., all being done by hand. The hay and other products are carried on the backs of men and women. In fact, the colonists were ignorant of all farming methods, except the care of cattle and the making of butter and cheese. A beginning under such conditions would have been most discouraging to a people less used to toil and privation. Without money, without skill, many thousands of miles from those on whom they had claims for assistance, it required the exercise of the firmest determination, courage, and faith, to hold out. Too much credit cannot be given to those in whom lay the care and direction of the colony, in its first efforts to take root. Almost daily they were called upon to administer comfort and aid on the one hand, and to reprove or arbitrate on the other. They performed the functions of teacher, physician, pastor, and judge, with patience and tact. In this connection, Messrs. Streiff, Duerst, and J.J. Tschudy, and Pastor Streissguth deserve special mention. Notwithstanding their efforts, however, there was much dissatisfaction and trouble for two or three years. If it had not been for the difficulty in returning home from so remote a place, and the utter want of means, it is more than likely that enough would have left and returned to Switzerland, or gone to other places, to breakup the colony. But most of them willingly or unwillingly accepted the situation, and made up their minds to win success.

After putting in their little crops, it was evident that something must be done to provide money for clothing and other necessaries, until the land should nourish the people. Many of the men, and also women, sought and found work elsewhere, — the men in the lead mines at Exeter and Mineral Point, and on the farms of the older settlers in the district; while the women engaged themselves as domestic servants, washerwomen, — in fact, doing anything by which they could honestly earn something. In those days, a mans wages were fifty cents and board per day, and even this small amount was paid mostly in flour, meat, potatoes, or other produce, which the Swiss workmen carried home on their shoulders, often as far as twenty-five miles. Money was then almost unknown in rural Wisconsin. In this way they contrived to live, until they could subdue enough land from which to win food at home.

When the colonists went into winter quarters at the close of the year 1845, Judge Nicholas Duerst returned to his native Switzerland, much to the regret of all. Upon his arrival home, the friends of the colony prevailed upon J. J. Tschudy to accept the position he had vacated. Mr. Tschudy arrived at the settlement in the autumn of 1846, and resided there until 1856, during which time he ably continued the work of his predecessor. By his judicious counsel and management, he won the approval and esteem not only of his countrymen but of all classes of people.

SELECTED BIBLIOGRAPHY

Luchsinger, John. "The Planting of the Swiss Colony at New Glarus, Wisconsin." *Collections of the State Historical Society of Wisconsin* 12 (1802): 335–382.

Luchsinger, John. "The Swiss Colony at New Glarus." *Collections of the State Historical Society of Wisconsin* 8 (1908): 431–445.

Ragatz, Lowell J., trans. and ed. "A Circuit Rider in the Old Northwest: Letters of the Reverend John H. Ragatz." *Wisconsin Magazine of History* 7 (1923–1924): 93–102.

Ragatz, Lowell Joseph, trans. and ed. "Memoirs of a Sauk Swiss. By the Rev. Oswald Ragatz." *Wisconsin Magazine of History* 19 (1935–1936): 182–227.

Ragatz, Lowell J., trans. and ed. "A Swiss Family in the New World: Letters of Jakob and Ulrich Bühler, 1847–1877." *Wisconsin Magazine of History* 6 (1922–1923): 317–333.

Rodolf, Theodore. "Pioneering in the Wisconsin Lead Region." *Collections of the State Historical Society of Wisconsin* 15 (1900): 338–389.

Schelbert, Leo, ed. *New Glarus 1845–1970: The Making of a Swiss American Town* (Glarus, Switzerland: Kommissionsverlag Tschudi & Co., AG, 1970).

Schelbert, Leo. "On Becoming an Emigrant: A Structural View of Eighteenth- and Nineteenth-Century Swiss Data." *Perspectives in American History* 7 (1973): 441–495.

Stuckey, Walter J. *The Hundredth Anniversary of the Swiss Evangelical and Reformed Church, New Glarus, Wisconsin* (New Glarus, WI, 1950).

Swiss-American Historical Society. *Prominent Americans of Swiss Origin* (New York: James T. White & Co., 1932).

Theiler, Miriam B. *New Glarus' First 100 Years* (Madison, WI: Campus Publishing Company, n.d.).

Tschudy, Millard. *New Glarus, Wisconsin: Mirror of Switzerland* (Monroe, WI: Monroe Evening Times, 1965).

Von Grueningen, John Paul. "Biography of J. J. von Grueningen." *Swiss American Historical Society Newsletter* 14 (February 1978): 12–21.

Von Grueningen, John Paul. *The Swiss in the United States* (Madison, WI: Swiss-American Historical Association, 1940).

INDEX

Page numbers referencing photos or illustrations are in *italic* type.

THE AUTHOR

Frederick Hale graduated from Macalester College in 1969 and was awarded master's degrees at Harvard University, the University of Minnesota, and the Johns Hopkins University. He received his Doctor of Philosophy at Johns Hopkins in 1976. He is the author of *Danes in Wisconsin* (revised in 2005) and *Swedes in Wisconsin* (revised in 2002), both published by the Wisconsin Historical Society Press. Hale has written four books in the field of Scandinavian immigration and has contributed articles to historical, literary, and theological journals in the United Kingdom, Scandinavia, Africa, and the United States.